Rejected by God

A near-death experience story of hope and truth and a word of warning for the curiously wayward Christian

By
Elizabeth Goodspeed

*Crystel —
God is love
Elizabeth
STAY BLESSED
John 4:8*

Rejected by God

Trilogy Christian Publishers A Wholly Owned Subsidiary of Trinity Broadcasting Network

2442 Michelle Drive Tustin, CA 92780

Rights Department, 2442 Michelle Drive, Tustin, CA 92780.

Trilogy Christian Publishing/TBN and colophon are trademarks of Trinity Broadcasting Network.

Cover design by: Grant Swank

For information about special discounts for bulk purchases, please contact Trilogy Christian Publishing.

Trilogy Disclaimer: The views and content expressed in this book are those of the author and may not necessarily reflect the views and doctrine of Trilogy Christian Publishing or the Trinity Broadcasting Network.

Manufactured in the United States of America

10 9 8 7 6 5 4 3 2 1

Library of Congress Cataloging-in-Publication Data is available.

ISBN: 978-1-63769-270-7

E-ISBN: 978-1-63769-271-4

To all my children:
Being your mom has given me strength beyond measure.

And

My loving husband, who faithfully worked to pay the bills while I
wrote this book.

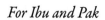

For Ibu and Pak

Contents

Preface

"...Lord, you know everything. You know that I love you." Jesus said,
"Then feed my sheep." John 21:17 (NLT)

To the reader:

For years, I recounted my story to others on an individual basis. Eventually, I could not continue telling my near-death experience (NDE) one by one. With the emotional support from my good friend Jenny, I began writing my experience to bear witness as to how our Triune God represents a God of love, mercy, and justice. As the world tries to tear us from our core Christian foundation through using what I believe inaccurate and politically motivated science, dark and exotic technology, and false life statements, those of us with NDEs have a testimony of the truth of God's other universe.

There is so much more than this earthly life. Every NDE holds a unique personal aspect, yet each contains similarities with which we can glean a basic concept of what it is like after we pass into the next phase of our lives. Eternal life continues beyond this life. Our minds and hearts travel to an alternate universe that is far more dynamic than earth life. As for my near-death, I experienced the dynamic light of God's glory rather than other's NDE of hell's fire and misery. For that, I am most grateful for God's mercy on my soul.

I feel the urgent need for people to recognize the times in which we are currently living. The day of the Lord is swiftly approaching. The world is getting darker and more chaotic with each passing day. Threats of violence to ourselves, our children, and our communities at large are a daily occurrence. Media images of clashes between governments, rioters, police, terrorist groups, and the average worker abound throughout the world. Nowadays, our children are exposed to multiple levels of violence in early childhood age, and the concept of towns like Mayberry is long gone, having dissolved into the waste bin of fictitious nonsense. We, as the world's population, have taken God out of all aspects of our lives in the name of science and technology and have lost ourselves amid it all. While science and technology can contribute to a greater quality of life, facilitating, among other things, such as clean water, medicine, and personal safety. It is the belief of no God that has allowed science and technology to become our god, and thus, inevitably, reducing the value of humanity to a mere subset of artificial intelligence.

This reduction of human value has humanity groaning for answers anywhere answers might be found. People feel angry, disenchanted, devalued, depressed, lost, lonely, imperfect, and underappreciated within our developed communities. We have turned the wrong way to combat these conditions and have mistakenly fallen to worship the false gods of alcohol, drugs, self-imagery, sex, and violence as a salve for our hurts. However, in so doing, we have created a deeper and darker problem where answers are never found, moreover, ignored. Only the God of hope, who walked on earth to teach humanity how to behave as one of His people, can solve humanity's crisis. We are victims of ourselves and our desires, defaulting into savages without morality. If you think this is not true, observe the behavior of people during a true pandemic. It was the Christian who stayed behind during the black plague to tend the sick. It was the Christian missionaries who worked in the Ebola-infested hospitals in the Congo.

Humankind creates a distance from the glory by refusing to acknowledge God as our creator, and we ignore putting His will at the top of our "to-do" list. When we deliberately choose to eliminate the God of love from our lives, evil ends up as the by-product. By definition, evil is the absence of love. For that reason, wherever there is no love, evil exists. Only love responds with truthful answers—the very thing humanity wants the most. Love conquers evil in all ways.

My hope is that my NDE story is an encouragement to others. It is not written to hurt or criticize individuals, rather reorient the heart of those who question the societal "truths" which leave them unable to make sense of it all. Expunging God from our educational systems and governments has created a void in humanity. All theories have become "a truth" as the world searches for an absolute truth. The laws of science and technology are constantly changing. Even the speed of light is no longer a constant. Where do people who search for absolute truth go? How do Christians, taught the truth of Jesus, depart from faith and gain more trust in scientific data than the Word of the Bible? How do those who have lost hope in life regain it?

More importantly, I want to stress that when you come to Jesus or turn back to the faith, Jesus will welcome you. Christianity is not filled with perfect individuals; it is overwhelmingly composed of people saddened by the world's fruitless gifts, who took a chance on Jesus and His story for humanity. Some people come to Jesus at an early age, whereas others join "the team" just before death. When you believe, I mean truly believe in Jesus, He claims you as His family; consequently gaining a new identity with this new family. You are no longer lost.

Blessings to all who seek the truth,
Elizabeth

This book is based on a real-life event.
Wherever possible, pseudonyms were used for
the protection of others.

"He that hath a wayward heart findeth no good..."
Proverbs 17:20 (ASV)

The Event

"But I count my life of no value to myself, so that I may finish my course and the ministry I received from the Lord Jesus, to testify to the gospel of God's grace." Acts 20:24 (HCSB)

Born a military brat and the youngest out of three children, I was endlessly having to deal with the constant fighting between my two older brothers, as anyone raised with headstrong boys would understand. Their constant fighting was usually to my demise since my parents always stuck me in between the two to reduce any conflict that might ensue. Regrettably, I had to sit in the middle of the backbench seat of the Buick station wagon, straddling the transmission hump, while my brothers fought around me in their individual quests to win some brainless argument. In the heat of the battle, the punches would inevitably land on me rather than the one intended. As a grown woman, I can honestly say I do not miss those years as my brothers' strategically positioned punching bag.

My dad was a career Army officer who embraced his family and loved his soldiers. Both my mom and dad were from Connecticut. My dad transplanted there from Maryland, but my mother and all her ancestors hailed from the nutmeg and surrounding states. Repeatedly, my mother would tell us how she was the first one to move away from the New England area since her ancestors arrived in the colonies in the mid-1600s. I am not quite certain if that was a fact or not, but the statement reinforced the point that she was perpetually living outside her natural comfort zone. Wherever the military sent my dad, my mother had to learn new acronyms, customs, foods, idioms,

13

and guidelines. The Army placed many demands on my mother, ones that most civilian moms never had to experience.

We moved frequently in the early years of my dad's career, with the average tour of duty being eighteen months to two years. My mom always tried to keep family customs alive by maintaining a routine. We went to the local post-schools during the weekdays. The weekends were filled with activities for growing families, such as soccer games, football practices, and piano lessons for my brothers. How I dreamed of having piano lessons like my brothers, but my mother chose to place me into ballet classes and Girl Scouts. I now understand that her intent was to give me activities that I could consider my own without brotherly competition. On Sundays, we dressed in our Sunday best and went to one of the post chapels for Protestant services.

My father was sent to Vietnam for his first combat tour just after I was born. I was ten months old when he was critically wounded and returned home for two years' worth of medical rehabilitation. After an incredible and miraculous period of healing, my father was placed back on active duty to continue on his career track. In November of 1968, just after my dad's second tour to Vietnam, my dad was assigned to Fort Monroe, Virginia, where we lived right on the Chesapeake Bay. Literally. We were assigned a three-bedroom, one-bath townhouse for quarters: 644 Gulick Drive was the first address I had to remember for school. Now long gone due to budget cuts, these quarters were condemned before we moved into them. When there were ferocious storms, the waves would break over the Chesapeake Bay wall and wash up on our front lawn, sometimes reaching the front door. During those storms, my mom would use every towel we owned to try and stop the seawater from entering the house. Regrettably, for the residents, sandbags were not an option for military quarters in those days.

My brothers shared a room where I was "forbidden" to enter, not that I genuinely wanted to be in their room anyway. It was filled with boy stuff, and who would want to play with that? One Christmas, my oldest brother, Ethan, received a radio as a gift. Now, that gift was different; it played music. I liked music. This was long before digital radios were available, and the analog tuning had to be just perfect to catch the radio station at its clearest point. One day, when both my brothers were out of the house for whatever reason, I sneaked into their room and found Ethan's radio. Purposefully looking at the dials as I made sure I knew which one was which, I found the on/off dial and rotated it to the "on" position. Darn. The sound emanating from the radio was nothing but talking. I quickly turned it off. Then, as I was walking out of their room, I remembered that the second dial allowed for other stations to come in for listening. I went back into their proscribed sanctuary and walked up to the radio. Click. The radio came on, and the talking was still there. I precisely measured exactly where the red line on the radio station "ruler" was so I could put the radio back to the original station without Ethan ever knowing. I knew the sting of sibling punishment would be eminent the exact time my brother found out I had been in his room, touching his radio. I gradually turned the tuning dial, and bingo! Music filled the room. Overjoyed with the sound emanating from the radio, I danced and danced in their room to the music until my legs were weak and my head spun. It was wonderful. When enough time had elapsed and cautious of their imminent return, I turned the tuner dial back to the original position, turned off the power dial, and, like a happy little camper, I skipped back to my room. None would be the wiser.

When my brother came home and found the radio station was "off" of its original station, he knew immediately I was the culprit. Moreover, I had two violations against me as a sibling—one for being in my brothers' room without an invite and one for touching his radio. Punishment was going to hurt. Ethan approached me as I was heading downstairs for dinner. "You went into my room and messed with my radio, didn't you?" I responded like any normal, well-raised American-blooded kid would—I lied. "No, I didn't!" "Yes, you did!"

he responded to my barefaced lie. My saving grace was that my mom was calling us both for dinner, so I rapidly slipped down the stairs and sat in my designated seat at the dining room table. Phew, I was safe for the time being, but I did not know what the future might hold in his retaliation for me.

The real question was, with the possibility of punishment lingering over my head, was playing with his radio worth it? Heck, yeah! However, knowing full well the consequences of his adolescent temper, I consciously chose to repeat this scenario only a few times in my life. Each time I went into my brothers' room to recapture that bliss of music, Ethan knew instinctively that I had been in his room. Astonishingly, he never, not once, sought retribution for my breaching the walls of his hallowed chamber and listening to the radio.

My dad was out of town a lot for his position with TRADOC, which left my mom as a single parent once again. When my mom went grocery shopping at the post commissary, my oldest brother, Ethan, was placed in charge of me and my other brother, Daniel. Post regulations stated that a ten-year sibling could be in a supervisory role to younger family members for a limited time each day. Parents anxiously waited for their oldest child to reach that tenth birthday, just to gain some desperately sought-after freedom to run some errands without a child on a hip, and mine were of no exception to this desire. Unfortunately, this provided Ethan a window of opportunity to take his frustrations out on Daniel and me.

As I have mentioned, Ethan in his adolescence possessed a blazing temper, which desperately needed parental monitoring. He would lash out at the most unwarranted times. When my mom said she was going to the commissary, I would proactively seek my friend Darla, who lived just a couple of houses down the street from us, so I was well out of the range of Ethan's war path and waited for my mother's return. Daniel would find one of the other boys to hang out with, just to dispel any conflict that might be brewing. We were not children who wanted to get into trouble, but it seemed as if trouble inevitably discovered us.

The times my friend Darla was not home and rainy days were days of pure discontent. I would intentionally hide in my room, away from any fighting in which Ethan and Daniel would engage while my mom was gone. Subsequently, the fight would spill over into my room, where my brother Ethan, in his rage, would take my bed pillow, knock me over on the floor and begin to suffocate me. This happened many, many times, with each time gaining duration. It happened so many times that I learned to quickly turn my head to either the right or left, where I could gather air at the crevasses of my shoulder as he would try to push the pillow across my face. I also learned quite quickly to lie limp as he forced the pillow tight to my face because my struggling would merely encourage him to exert more pressure. It was pure conditional training on steroids. I remember being so dizzy when he would eventually release the pillow from my head that I could hardly sit up and would just lay on the floor a minute or two to squelch the spin.

Routinely, following the suffocation episode, he would shout at me, "God, I wish I had a gun so I could kill you." I would say back to him, "Why? You almost did with a pillow." To this, he replied, "Yeah, but a gun would be so much better." He would then land a few punches on me, warn me of an impending doom if I told anyone, and quickly exit the room. As one would imagine, potential death by suffocation and gunshot are big fears of mine, even to this day. It is amazing that young children can instinctively learn how to work their bodies to fight the dangers of harm coming to them, just as I did. I have seen in videos where babies in the womb during an abortion exhibit signs of manipulating their bodies to get out of harm's way as they are defending their own lives. The fight for life occurs naturally within all of us.

In 1972, while at the Naval Command and Staff College in Norfolk, VA (my dad was selected to attend the school as a cross military service student), my father was "volun-told" to a position in the embassy in Jakarta, Indonesia. (I use the hyphenated term "volun-told" because, in theory, it was a volunteer position, but in reality, he could not turn down the assignment.) I was ten years old, and the world was in chaos. The ongoing Vietnam War, hijacking of commercial airplanes to Cuba, and the travesty of Northern Ireland's bedlam flooded the national TV airwaves, and the Army was sending our family to a remote assignment, away from the safety of our American borders. Without hesitation, my parents went into high gear, donating expendable household goods, storing needed items that could not be sent overseas, and packing the small number of goods to be sent to Southeast Asia that would be a necessity for this tropical assignment.

I remember flying into Travis Air Force base from Tampa after we had spent some time with my grandparents in Florida. It was at Travis that we were to catch a flight to Honolulu, Hawaii. The thought of going to Hawaii would have been exciting if it had not been for the constant threats of hijacking. The packed flight was filled with brand-new soldiers, having just graduated from basic training and heading to Saigon. By default, my dad was the senior-ranking officer on the chartered flight, a position of which was most undesired at the time. During the entire flight over the Pacific Ocean, I was in a severe panic for fear the plane would be hijacked and I would be stuck in Cuba for the rest of my life. At my age, I did not know the politics of the Cuban communist uprising; I just knew that I did not know any Spanish, and the thought of armed passengers shoving the end of a weapon in my face did not seem like a jolly good time.

My fear of hijacking consumed me so much that I threw up the lunch my mother forced me to eat in the airport cafeteria prior to the Honolulu flight. We had a significant wait time until the subsequent leg of our overseas journey, so my mother, not knowing when the next possibility for food, nor the quality of it, required all of us to eat lunch before our next boarding. I kept insisting that I was not hungry and that there was nothing on the cafeteria line that even looked remotely appetizing. At my mother's insistence on having at least something in my stomach, I chose a bowl of peaches and a vanilla milkshake. It was an overwhelmingly wrong choice of food because by the time we finished lunch and paused to do some airport gift shopping, I mentioned to my mom that I was not feeling well and was in desperate need of a ladies' restroom. My mom declared it was down the hallway to the left. I scurried out with my mom right on my heels. Halfway down the hallway, with the ladies' restroom sign in sight, I broke out into a full sprint, trying to make it to the bathroom before my lunch resurfaced. I entered the ladies' room, opened the closest stall door when I proceeded to bend over in the hopes that my projectile vomit would make the porcelain toilet. Nope! Missed it by a couple of inches. There I stood, heaving my cookies all over the bathroom floor, drenching my shoes and socks with the smelly sourness of my undigested lunch.

My mother was raised in an older generation where respect for people's jobs mattered no matter what job they had. Nowadays, people leave public spaces compromised by their trash and waste. Not knowing how long it might be before the janitorial staff could get in to clean, my mother took the time to clean the bathroom floor after my mess because she knew others had to use the restroom. More importantly, my mother knew she had bigger problems that she needed to address after the discharge of my lunch. We were going to be on a thirteen-hour plane flight with my clothes smelling like vomit. What poor traveler would want to sit next to that? The smell would be enough for the entire planeload of travelers to grab "the sick bag conveniently located in the seat pocket in front of them" and be sick themselves. My mother tried to clean the front of my dress as best as she could and asked me to take off my socks and shoes. She washed my shoes—literally, with the provided bathroom hand soap. Then proceeded to wash my socks in the same manner. With a couple of hours of layover still on our travel agenda, my mom asked security for an outdoor bench, such as one that airport personnel might use for break time. The news of my loose lunch episode had rapidly traveled throughout our area of the concourse, and the staff was more than willing to send me outside for a bit.

Sitting on a second story bench located just outside the passenger loading ramp in the hot California sun, my mom and I sat waving my white socks in the air, the skirt of my wet dress spread out across my thighs, as my shoes were splayed wide apart in the hope that everything would dry (and have no smell) before we boarded our upcoming flight. We watched as pilots, crew members, and baggage handlers prep the outgoing planes. In our unique position, we had an eye-level view of the activities inside the cockpit of the parked planes. As we sat there, one of the planes began to taxi out, and through the cockpit window, we could read the lips of the pilot, who turned to the co-pilot and asked, "What is she doing?" Knowing the situation, one of the flight attendants leaned over, whispered something in the pilot's ear, and the following word we saw the pilot say was "Ohhh..." My mom merely smiled a big smile that said, "you just don't know my pain" as she gave a quick farewell wave to the pilot. To this day, I cannot stand the taste of milkshakes.

Landing in Hawaii at midnight did not allow us much opportunity to appreciate the beauty of the island before we were on the next leg of our journey: Guam. After Guam, we landed in Saigon to unload the active-duty passengers. It was a sad sendoff since the crew and my dad experienced the conditions many of these new soldiers were going to face. As I mentioned, my dad had already done two tours in Vietnam and was acutely aware of the dangers at hand. At the time of our flight, the North Vietnamese army had advanced to the proximity of the airport in an attempt to capture it. In a counter-offensive move, the South Vietnamese army fired artillery off the end of the runway. I can legitimately say I was in the Vietnam War at the ripe old age of ten. The pilot thought my dad and mom were absolutely insane for bringing the family into a war zone and walked down the plane aisle to chastise my parents for doing so. The pilot abruptly stopped his reprimanding after my dad had presented him his set of orders and a copy of the plane tickets issued from the US Army. Not being able to promise the safety of our take-off, the pilot informed my dad that he would do his best clearing the end of the runway without getting hit. Once the active-duty service members were fully disembarked and their gear unloaded, the pilot and crew shut up the plane and took off without any tarmac prep for the following leg of the flight to Singapore. From Singapore, it was a brief flight into Jakarta.

Life was arduous in Indonesia for a family coming from a developed country, and our family was no exception. That is not to say just Americans found it difficult. No, it was equally problematic for those coming from England, the Netherlands, or any other western industrialized country. The commodities available in our countries of origin just did not exist in Indonesia.

Indonesia was and is the largest Muslim country in the world. Relatively new in its independence in 1972, the capital city of Jakarta was still learning how to manage infrastructure development while maintaining the increasing demands of a high level of unemployed and undereducated population. We learned to live without water and electricity for extended periods of time. My mom became well-versed in home remedies for our health and nutritional needs.

We attended the embassy school unimaginatively named the Joint Embassy School (JES). School was an hour-long, hot bus drive to Chelandak, a suburb of the capital city of Jakarta. Exceptionally constructed and unique in its design, JES used futuristic geometric pods for classrooms with connecting covered sidewalks. Years later, when I was in college, I learned that the school had burned down due to arson. From my understanding, the person(s) was never apprehended. It was unfortunate, since I possess fond memories of good friends and dedicated teachers in those classrooms that others will never have.

We were not citizens of Indonesia; therefore, attending a local public school was forbidden to us. It would have been too much of a financial burden for the community, which was already struggling to educate its people. I think my parents were relieved to know that our western education would be continued in light of the limited educational opportunity in Jakarta. If Indonesians wished to attend and their families could afford the tuition at JES, they were more than welcome to enroll in school with us. In fact, there was a substantial scholarship fund for local residents to tap into for tuition assistance if needed. As a result, we had a significant number of Indonesians that attended school with us.

I rather enjoyed going to JES because it was sponsored by four different countries (American, Australian, British, and Czechoslovakian), which provided us a multi-faceted education. Our population was a beautifully diversified international body of students. The Aussies and the Brits would study for their A and O level exams, while the Americans studied for the SATs. As the students from Eastern Europe arrived with limited English skills, we would pair up to help them to overcome the language barrier since all classes at the school were taught in English. The Eastern European students would always reciprocate by sharing their higher level of math and science skills with our homework assignments. When Queen Elizabeth II came for a visit in 1974, all of our British Commonwealth friends were given an excused day off for a chance to see her while the rest of us "yanks" attended school. We did not mind, though. They ribbed us about possibly regretting the American Revolution, and we pushed back with having a better fourth of July than they do. It was all done in good fun.

Since Indonesia rests in the tropics along the equator, one of the awesome things about life there is year-round swimming. While my parents enjoyed playing tennis with my brothers, I loved to swim. One summer, the American Club organized a fantastic summer program for all the kids during the break. It included all sorts of activities, from theater, basketball, soccer, arts and crafts, hula dancing, ping-pong, and guitar lessons to whatever the adult population knew just enough of and cared to teach us while on vacation.

My favorite activity was synchronized swimming. The coach, whom I believe was one of the wives in the Foreign Service Department, had been a synchronized swimmer in college and was willing to teach a routine to a bunch of willing school-aged girls. I fell in love with the sport. I enjoyed it so much better than being on a swim team, where stroke perfection is required to compete against the clock and others in the pool. (Moreover, my dad was co-captain of his college swim team and, in his love for me, would have overanalyzed every inch of my stroke.) On the other hand, synchronized swimming was a combination of dancing and swimming to a musical beat. I was planning to be the next Ester Williams, even though I did not have a clue as to who she was. I could get lost in an underworld of water by performing flips, suspended handstands, kicks, turns, and basic routine moves, all while holding my breath. As those who participate in the sport know, breath control is a critical skill for synchronized swimmers. There is a lot of submerged activity in setting up the routine above the waterline, and an excellent pair of lungs is a necessity. It was a world where my brothers could not, nor would not, compete with me. I was alone in my physical achievements and failures, while my adolescent heart did not have a care in the world.

Around my 13th birthday, I was swimming at the American Club outdoor pool, practicing my underwater handstands as long as my breath allowed. Ethan, who was at the pool with me, spotted me in the water with my legs protruding up in the air above the water's surface and decided to play an ill-fated trick. Slowly and quietly so as I was not alerted to his presence, he entered the water where I was practicing my aquatic gymnastics and stood next to my inverted body. Like a cat ready to pounce, he waited for the precise moment when the back of my head was crowning the surface of the water. He then placed his hand on top of my wet head and forced me further under the water, holding me there for as long as he so desired. I felt the weight of his hand on my head and the pressure of his fingers squeezing the sides of my skull to maintain domination of me as I struggled for control under the water. *Oh no*, I thought, *here we go again!* Unfortunately, this time it was not a pillow.

I desperately remember trying to remove his hand from my head without any success. The span of his hand practically covered the entire backside of my head. Fully submersed, I would raise my right hand and attempt to knock his hand off my head without victory. Then I would extend my left hand to try to hit his hand in an attempt to release the pressure of his control. Eventually, I gave up and laid limp in the water just like I would when he had the pillow over my face on my bedroom floor. I retained no air, and I was becoming weak very quickly. Laying unresponsively in the water, I knew I needed to conserve my energy to lower my legs to the pool floor and push my head above the water's surface to inflate my lungs with much desired and required air. However, this time without air was different, and I could feel the difference. He was older and bigger and possessed far more strength than the boy of ten, taking out his aggressions on me in my bedroom. Even in my stillness, my brother refused to let go of my head and kept applying pressure to restrain me under the water.

My initial location of pain was marked in my chest wall. My rib cage began to hurt from the inside out, much like the pain from incredible bruising on the inside of your chest wall. I could not breathe through the pain; I possessed no air, so I laid there with his hand on my head, keeping me submerged under the water. It was an odd sensation. Typically, when a balloon is inflated with enormous amounts of air, it pops loudly at the point of exceeding its stretched capacity. When I thought my chest was going to burst from the lack of oxygen, I found the opposite true. With the *lack* of air, my lungs felt as if they were at the point of exploding.

In every moment of the situation, my will to live was active, as I was trying to figure out a way to fight off the impending drowning event. As I was physically and psychologically managing the intense pain in my chest, my brain began to experience intense pressure, as if it was going to explode as well. The pain had traveled from my chest to my head. A thank you to all my science teachers, as I now knew at the age of thirteen, that the effects from the lack of oxygen had directly traveled to my brain. Although grateful that my chest had stopped hurting, I recognized I was in deeper trouble in my efforts to save my life since the agony was presently in my head. I have never felt pain like that before nor since this accident. It felt as if all the nooks and crannies of my brain had swelled with the lack of oxygen and was pushing my skull outward. It was such an intense feeling; I still recall it to this day. Dying is painful.

When people pass out, they usually remember the last thing that happened, and then the next memory will be the one waking up, typically with someone shouting their name. For example, I have heard scuba divers describe passing out under the water. When recalling their last activity, they can remember some mishap occurring, then awakening to finding themselves on the deck with team members or instructors shouting at them. It is as if there was a splice of time taken from their memory bank. That is not what happened to me. I remember everything that happened in detail. I remember my feelings and emotions. I can recall all the questions I formulated in my mind because my mind was intensely alive and working.

As my submerged body was giving up on its earthly life, I remember beseeching God to take the hurt away, and *instantly* the pain was gone. Nevertheless, I found myself in complete and total darkness. My mind was hastily trying to analyze the situation. In fact, I think because I was pain-free, my mind was working exceedingly well. I tried to figure out my orientation in the space I found myself, but I could not observe my hands, my feet, nor any part of my body. I was in *absolute darkness*. I knew I was no longer in the water anymore and relieved of pain, but I was also completely disoriented as to where I was. As my brain processes were working overtime trying to gather the environmental information around me, I became acutely aware that I was in a void of some type. There was no air, per se, in that there was no smell, no feeling of a breeze, no weight of heat, no type

25

of atmospheric compression against my body. There was no sound or sensation of vibrations. I could not taste or smell anything, such as minerals or airborne particulates. When I looked down to see my arms and hands, they were not visible. My feet were not standing on anything, though, curiously, I did not feel as if I was suspended. Your body may not cross over, but your mind sure does!

The Bible warns us about the darkness, and I can tell you it is a solitary and depressing state of being. I did the only thing I knew to do. I called out to God and asked Him, "God, how do I get out of here?" *Instantly*, a tiny pinprick of light was visible to my lower right side. Now, things were different. Now my mind could process the void on a different level. What joy and elation I had in seeing the light, as small as it was. Most critically, I now had an orientation. I had a "here" and a "there." I now had a goal, an objective to achieve.

In the darkness, with my new goal in mind, I encountered a more serious problem. I could not move. I could not see nor feel my feet, let alone feel a floor or wall. It was just space. As I write this today, I wonder what applied theoretical quantum physics would designate this place? The Bible calls it the darkness.

Adamant that I was not going to stay in the darkness, I began to try to figure out how to move to the light. Physical movement was out of the question. I pleaded with God to show me how to get to the light. Nothing happened. Experiencing no sensation of time, I just stayed in the darkness, looking at this tiny speck of light. Naively, I tried to come up with actions that would please God and aid my progress. I tried arranging my words perfectly for the "perfect prayer" because perfectly worded prayers will get you what you want, right? Wrong! I did not move one bit. I tried reciting the 23rd Psalm as best my thirteen-year-old memory could recall. I tried to remember some of the prayers we said in Sunday School over and over again. Nothing. I kept trying to switch up the words of my prayer. I even resorted to begging. "Pleeeeease. Pretty Pleeeease." Nothing. Nevertheless, I became determined not to let the darkness beat me. Since there was no idea of time (or there was all the time in the world, depending on how I could look at it), I was adamant I was going to the light. I was going to figure this out no matter how long it took. My mind was processing the situation, just as I would have processed my math or spelling test. Interestingly, when someone crosses over, their mind transfers with them. I had the same mental analytical processing skills that I had on earth. The little voice in your head stays with you forever. One fact about death is a person does not lose that unique inner voice; rather, it is amplified.

Ultimately, I became so exhausted with my prayer formation that I stopped creating prayers in my brain and began to plead to God with deep love in my heart, *God and Jesus, I just want to be with you. I want to go to the light.* That was the game-changer. Whammo! I started to move to the light. It was a floating sensation. I moved with purpose and direction, without using my arms and legs. It was as if my heart was directing my body to float to the light. Then I stopped. What? What happened? I was not moving, then I was, and then I stopped! What gives? Utilizing my analytical skills to assess what just happened, I tried to reenact all the previous steps I did to manage myself moving again. Like the methodical steps in completing a 3D cubed puzzle, I repeated the words of the prayers and the scripture again. No movement. Did I get the words wrong? Becoming frustrated again, I went back to centering the feeling of knowing and loving God in my heart, and I restarted my ascension to the light.

I have to laugh at this point in my story because in mid-flight, I started to giggle. The feeling of "fly-floating" is a delightful sensation. Nothing like the carnival rides you have at the local state fairs. You feel absolutely no pressure against your body. There is no wind, no sense of hot or cold, no smell, just movement to the light. The traveling sensation fostered in me a sense of great joy at the prospect of leaving a dark void of all things and revealing what was on the other side of this adventure. My giggling threw me off focus from what my heart was feeling to get me to move in the first place, and I began to slow down. Oops! I had to refocus and get my heart back to concentrating on how much I loved God and wanted to see Him. It was then that I realized it was not the words that launched the next world to me; it was my heart for Jesus that crossed me over to the light. The Bible mentions the darkness 166 times in the New International Version (NIV) translation and talks about the heart and its condition 532 times. It is our heart's condition that draws God near to us, never what we do or say.

As I traveled closer to the light, the light became warm and inviting. The light was a cross between a light for direction (as with a flashlight) and a glow of being. Once the light was all around me and the darkness was long gone, I felt love almost instantly. The light was love. I knew the light was Yahweh, Elohim, the God who created all things. I possessed an innate knowledge that the light was God the Father, God the Son, and God the Holy Spirit. I knew the love coming from the light was my Creator and that I belonged to the light. It was joyful and glorious. There was a sense of going home and a reconnection to truth and pure love.

The amount of love grew exponentially as I traveled closer to the light, and the closer I traveled to the light, the faster I seemed to fly. As I traveled to the light, my heart was calling out to God, as only a heart could do, telling Him that He was wonderful. All I could do was praise God with every cell of my being as I was traveling to Him. It was as if that was the only thing my heart could do. I heard heavenly beings singing, glorifying God in surround sound. At that moment, it sounded as if the angels and all the heavenly beings were singing *with* me as I ascended. It was as if that was the natural state of my heart. Praising Him was instinctive, like a non-voluntary reflex in our human body. I felt peace and at home. It was Glorious. In my heavenly climb, I felt myself becoming a part of the light as if being welcomed to a bigger community of life. This convergence of energy, mine and God's, granted me a sense of overwhelming love. No wonder most people with near-death experiences never want to leave.

As my energy was glorifying and uniting with God, and the light grew to about ten feet in diameter in front of me, I was thrown off course to the right side of the light "tunnel." There, I found myself once again in a darkened space. It was different from the first darkness. In this darkness, I had a feeling that it was massive, yet I could not tell you the dimensions. I had a sense that there were many others there like me, yet I could not see them. Once more, I could not identify a ceiling, floor, or walls. It was a darkened, grand "space-like" place that seemed the size of many football fields. I had no fear of being in it, not like the first darkness that was a void of all things.

I watched as an elderly man in a white robe approached me. My initial thought was that he was my maternal grandfather, who had passed away just a couple of years earlier. As the man came closer to me, I realized it was not my grandfather, yet I knew I knew him. Instinctively knowing I was assigned to his team, I knew this man was of considerable importance. Desperate to recall his name, I began to have the sixth sense that there were others there for me as well, though I did not see them. The gentleman informed me that I needed to return. I flatly refused, and he laughed at me, saying, "No. No. You need to go back." I can remember thinking, remember my mind was working just fine, "No. I am going to go to God." I point blank refused his offer of my earthly return and firmly told him no. He reiterated his statement that I needed to go back because there was more for me to do. Once more, I flatly refused. (What happens next is rather difficult to explain; the mechanics of my mind were still earthbound in many ways, but I no longer sustained my body for movement. Everything was performed by thoughts and feelings because I was energy at this point.) My mind used to manipulating a human body, which I no longer had, used my left arm "movement" to emphasize that I was going to go to God and stay there, because God is love and I was going to love. The man insisted I needed to return and do more here on Earth. I threw a tantrum in front of him and shouted, "No! No, I am not! I am not going to go back there! That is not love! I am not going back to that family. I am going to love! I am going to God," and at this point, I attempted to stomp my no longer existing right foot. He had enough of my uncooperative behavior and shouted, "Go! Go back now!" I screamed, "Noooooooooo!" all the way back through the "tunnel" and into my body. This does not mean it was an actual tunnel, rather, the passageway to my return back into my human body had a tunnel-like quality to it.

I felt and saw my legs touch the floor of the pool. Instinctively, my torso was raised out of the water as if someone was lifting it out. My brother was long gone as I readjusted to my surroundings. My body was so *heavy* and extraordinarily difficult to move. A woman jumped into the water and swam over to assist me. Never inquiring as to her name, nor did she offer it to me, she asked me if I was okay. I nodded, coughing up water and moaning in deep muscular pain as I tried moving my body.

I have a confession to make at this point in my story. When the woman asked me if I was okay, I looked at her bathing suit and thought, *Oh my! You need to go shopping.* To my surprise, this kind woman coming to my rescue was wearing a massively outdated swimsuit. (I felt I was trapped in the movie scene of *It's a Wonderful Life* with Jimmy Stewart, where the angel Clarence had just rescued George Bailey from the icy waters beneath a drawbridge and proceeded to dry their cold, wet clothing in the bridge operator's office. George Bailey and the drawbridge operator look strangely at Clarence's old-fashioned wet underwear attire hanging on the makeshift clothesline.[1]) As this woman was helping me replace oxygen in my lungs, I realized the error of my inner thoughts and secretly admonished myself for being so critical of a Good Samaritan. To my defense, in 1975, the swim fashion of the day were speedos and bikinis, and my rescuer's suit had to have been straight out of the 1930s. I rest my case.

As I was heaving loudly for desperate life-giving quantities of air, the woman said she was there to help me adjust back to earth and back into my body. The pain of regaining air in my lungs was searing.

It is funny how this earthly body works. It hurts to lose air, and it hurts to regain air. My body felt like it had the weight of a fully grown elephant on top of it. She informed me that I would rapidly adjust to the weight of my body and that the heaviness would dissipate. Once I was breathing somewhat normally and could move my aching body, my rescuer told me she had to go. I painfully nodded my head in understanding as I looked around the pool for my brother.

Meanwhile, the lifeguard was pacing on the pool deck, hastily blowing his whistle at me because it was "break" time, and he wanted me out of the pool. As I was standing in the waist-deep water and clueless as to how long I had been submerged, I turned back to my rescuer again to say a heartfelt thank you, but she was gone. Again, I mentally reprimanded myself for being hyper-critical of her bathing suit and not uttering a word of thanks. Here, this woman was trying to help me, and I was critical of her clothing! Ugh, I still regret it to this day. More importantly, I genuinely believe the woman was my guardian angel, and I am grateful to her for her assistance.

I am not upset with my brother for his cruel trick. We have all snared someone into a deceitful situation. Throughout my life, my brother was kind, considerate, and extremely supportive of me. In fact, I am honored I was able to see the other side and know that Jesus is the way, the truth, and the life. It was my "Joseph-down-the-well" moment. Wonderfully, I derived the greatest pleasure in chronicling this story to my mother during her last hospital stay, six months before she went home to be with Jesus. For me to tell my mother what to expect and to prepare her for the transition before she died represents a cherished moment I will always harbor in my heart.

Does my story tell you the interior of heaven and its streets paved with gold? In a word, no. I do not think that is my earthly assignment. I believe I am to warn about the darkness and the centering of your heart as my "more for me to do." There are other individuals with an NDE story that have a more extensive description of heaven's abode. More importantly, I think we desperately want to place earthly items in our picture of God's house. Fortunately, God's house does not require earthly items. The book of Revelation talks about lamp posts and a New Jerusalem; however, these represent earthly qualities for an earthly perspective. I know heaven is grander than anything earth could possibly offer; regrettably, I lack the descriptive vocabulary to depict it. When I was traveling in the light, I no more cared about the earth and earthly things because I had the source of all things in front of me. In Genesis 28, Jacob beholds angels going up and down a ladder. Heaven is interactive *with* us. In Acts 7:55, Stephen saw the glory of God as I did in my experience. Philippians 3:20 reports our citizenship is in heaven, and that is exactly how I felt. In John 8:12, Jesus spoke of being the light, and whoever follows Him shall never walk in darkness. *This is truth.*

The darkness I experienced was desolate. I never want to go back to it, and I definitely do not want any of you to experience it either. If I could not withstand the darkness and had to cry out to God to reveal to me how to get out, then I cannot even imagine the desolation and pain of hell. Please, I beg of you, if you believe in Jesus, make sure it is a belief of the heart, not of words or academic understanding. The dynamics where He resides are different from ours. Earth has limitations placed upon it. When we expect God to conform to our understanding, then we limit His abilities to do for us as He so chooses. I encounter so many people who are keenly focused on quoting scripture to gain a heavenly admission ticket; unfortunately, it is not the knowledge of scripture that gets you into heaven. I tried using scripture memorization as an entrance permit, and it did not work. It was the focus of my heart and knowing I loved God that allowed me to go to Him. It is imperative everyone understands you must create your own love language for God. No one can do it for you. The Bible is to help direct you to know and love God. Scripture encourages us to recognize who God is and where we fit in God's design for us, but it is not in lieu of your heart for God. Only you can decide whether you are going to believe and love God or not. It is my fervent prayer that this book helps you decide to have a relationship with Jesus and God. A life with God is bigger and better than you can imagine. As a person with an NDE, I implore you to know that the God of the Christian Bible represents the God of truth. Earthly life is short and complicated. Heavenly life is complete and eternal.

The Darkness

"They grope in darkness with no light; He makes them stagger like drunkards." Job 12:25 (NIV)

Here on earth, the dream vacation is going somewhere doing absolutely nothing. No schedules. No meetings. No appointments. Just live and let live. I remember my vacation to St. Augustine, FL, the year my daughter was newly commissioned in the US Army. The previous four years had consisted of racing down to Florida from Missouri to move her out of her dorm and place all her belongings into a storage locker every springtime, just to turn around and pull all her belongings out of storage and move her into her new dorm each fall. (Of course, she changed dorms every year she was in college—a challenge to our stamina as aging parents!) I would bitterly complain I just wanted a trip to Florida that did not consist of racing around and repeatedly having something to do and be somewhere. Each time, when we returned to Missouri after several days of exhausting work in the Florida sunshine, people would inevitably ask if we had a good time. No! It was exhausting. Finally, my nephew's wedding in St. Augustine, FL, allowed us a relaxing wedding vacation. We did not have a care in the world except to attend the church wedding at six p.m. on a warm Saturday night. Ah! It was bliss. No worries, just sleeping, eating, and relaxing. The void of doing nothing on a vacation is completely different from *the void of darkness*.

I am here to inform you that the darkness exists. It is real. It is an urgent warning to you, your family, and friends. I have been there and do not want to go back. It is an abandoned place where you cannot identify a thing, not even your hand in front of your face.

When I lived in Colorado, I considered my hand at spelunking, aka "cave exploring." The cold, wet earth, with its underground caverns and the protrusions of stalagmites and stalactites, really did not strike my fancy. The constant exposure to underground wetness, feet slipping from underneath you as you descend further into the pitch blackness, dirt getting into every wrinkle of your skin, and the fear of getting trapped did not make me feel invigorated. After a few attempts and coming to realize the cute single guys are swimmers, my recreational activities as a cave explorer abruptly ended. Nonetheless, those that have experience as a spelunker can understand how dark the depths of the earth become when exploring a cave's passageways deep underground when your flashlight goes out. You lack your sense of direction and can only rely on feeling your way around. Pitch blackness makes you desperate for a smell or a brush of air to help guide you on your journey in the cave.

I tell you, the darkness was more dreadful than any darkness I experienced while underground, with no visible light. There was no feeling of walls, ceiling, or floor. I could not feel anything with my hands or my feet, nor could I feel any sense of temperature or air movement. It was a total void of all things, and it is *frightening*.

When I initially entered the darkness, I was confused. I tried figuring out where I was but failed. There was no sound, no feeling, no smell, no taste, no sight; it was a negated existence of all senses. From what I could discern, I was completely estranged from everything. It was a total pitch-blackness, and it was terribly real. Thankful that I was no longer in pain from the suffocation of drowning, I tried to move, but I moved nowhere because there was nowhere there. Without a geographical surrounding, nor a sense of up or down, in or out, there was no here or there. As I lasted in the darkness, a sense of intense distress overcame me. I tried to move again, but where? I cannot feel a floor below me, a ceiling above me, nor any walls beside me. There was no airflow to follow. As I said, it was just a dark void of everything. I did not sense I was in the pit of hell since there was no sound, fire, or anything most people would associate with hell. Instead, I was in a state of emptiness with an *exceedingly active mind.*

You would think that a void in your life would be relaxing, like our wedding holiday, but this was completely different. There was no one and nothing, and it was lonely and scary. As I lingered in the blackness with my mind racing, trying to figure out my situation, my discomfort progressed to fear. Fear because there were no answers to my questions. Fear because there was no one. Fear because I had nowhere to go and did not know where I was.

All of us have to deal with a "darkness." We all own dark clouds in the skyline of our lives. For some, the dark cloud comes and goes; for others, the cloud of despair and trials comes and lingers over us for what seems an eternity. Only through our cries for help and focus on Jesus as our Lord and Savior can we manage the times of trials. When we accept Christ in our hearts, we know that our life with trials is short compared to eternity in heaven with our Creator God. First Peter 1:6 (NIV) declares, "In all this you greatly rejoice, though now for a little while you may have had to suffer grief in all kinds of trials." Our hope is in Jesus and the message He brought to the world. The Apostle James puts the world and our lives into perspective. This life is not all that we have. There is more to it, and when we concentrate on life in the light that is to come for all those who believe, then we are able to manage the darkness better. James 1:2-4 (NIV) says, "Consider it pure joy, my brothers and sisters, whenever you face trials of many kinds, because you know that the testing of your faith produces perseverance. Let perseverance finish its work so that you may be mature and complete, not lacking anything."

Our God warns us about the darkness many times in the Bible. It is a dreadful place. If we do not consciously choose to love God and follow the guidelines God places on us through the Ten Commandments (reduced to two by Jesus: love God and love your neighbor), we subsequently choose the darkness. Moses said to the people, "Do not be afraid. God has come to test you, so that the fear of God will be with you to keep you from sinning" (Exodus 20:20, NIV).

God does not want people to experience the darkness on the other side. People need to know that God exists and that the God of our Bible is a faithful and life-giving God. As Christians, if we choose not to live a life showing the world how Christ works in our lives, we choose to deliver people over to this darkness. When we do not inform people of the loving, saving grace of our Lord, not only do we send people to the darkness, but we possibly also send ourselves. God cautions Ezekiel about his role as a prophet:

> If I say to the wicked person, "You will surely die," but you do not warn him—you don't speak out to warn him about his wicked way in order to save his life—that wicked person will die for his iniquity. Yet I will hold you responsible for his blood. But if you warn a wicked person and he does not turn from his wickedness or his wicked way, he will die for his iniquity, but you will have saved your life. Now if a righteous person turns from his righteousness and practices iniquity, and I put a stumbling block in front of him, he will die. If you did not warn him, he will die because of his sin and the righteous acts he did will not be remembered. Yet I will hold you responsible for his blood. But if you warn the righteous person that he should not sin, and he does not sin, he will indeed live because he listened to your warning, and you will have saved your life.

> Ezekiel 3:18-21 (HCSB)

This is critical information. My NDE presented me a gift to deliver to people, Christian and non-Christian alike. Life exists beyond this earthly realm. While we are on earth, everyone must decide on a belief system, whatever one that may be. It is that belief system that will endure eternal consequences. For non-Christians,

I hope my NDE will give pause and contemplation of an alternate worldview, allowing for the truth of God's love to come into fruition.

For those who profess Jesus Christ, we will be recognized by the fruit our faith produces. In the book of Matthew, Jesus advises us, "Many will say to Me on that day, 'Lord, Lord, did we not prophesy in Your name, and in Your name drive out demons and perform many miracles?' Then I will tell them plainly, 'I never knew you; depart from Me, you workers of lawlessness!'" (Matthew 7:22-23, NIV) I, as a Christian who knows the light, must counsel people of the impending darkness to come upon the world. The place where souls are confined to a nothingness, where the absence of everything is hauntingly lonely. I was terrified. This place can be escaped by everyone. The time is limited and getting more limited by the day. Everyone's earthly days are numbered. No one knows the hour set aside for them to meet God Almighty. Before that day arrives, I want to tell everyone about the wonderful loving, saving grace of Jesus Christ. John 8:12 (NIV) informs us, "when Jesus spoke again to the people, he said, 'I am the light of the world. Whoever follows me will never walk in darkness but will have the light of life.'"

The Light

"The true Light who gives light to every man was coming into the world." John 1:9 (NIV)

In the 1970s, singer-songwriter Randy Newman sang his hit song "Short People," and my mother would repeatedly sing that song to my face, especially when it played on the radio. My mother gained her five feet six inches height early in her youth and was teased nonstop for being the tallest girl in her class until she was in high school. The constant teasing left an emotional mark on my mother's heart, so when I came up two inches shorter than her, my mother sought out her revenge by teasing me every time that senseless song played on the radio. Argh, how I despise that song! Nevertheless, I learned how to use my more diminutive stature to my advantage. For example, when I clean the house. If any dirt or dust exists above my line of sight, in reality, it does not exist. Right? Moreover, if it does not exist, then I do not have to clean it. *Woot! Woot!* That is, until my six-foot-tall husband points it out, at which point I hand him the dust rag. Well, my husband does not like cleaning, so he learned a long time ago, not to mention the dirt well above my head. This scenario worked well for years until one day, my friend Sherrie, who stands a solid five feet ten inches, looked up at my kitchen ceiling fan blades and mentioned how dirty they were. She was not being rude, just honest. I, in turn, gave her a dust cloth to clean the top of the fan blades when, to my embarrassment, I realized the dirt was so caked on that she could not wipe it off. Consequently, I periodically get the kitchen step stool, reach my short, little arms up to the top of the fan blades and wipe them off, as well as all my photo frames, cabinets, doorframes, and the such.

Heaven is like this. Not that heaven is dirty and needs a thorough cleaning, but that it exists out of our line of sight. Even though we cannot see it or touch it, it is a reality beyond our earthly vision. It existed before earth's creation. God's unseen realm existed prior to the earth because it was from heaven that Elohim spoke the world and all its particulates into reality.

In the book of Job, after Job has stated his case and replied to his friends' negative discourse on God, the Lord responds to Job in chapter thirty-eight.

> Where were you when I laid the earth's foundation? Tell me, if you understand. Who marked off its dimensions? Surely you know! Who stretched a measuring line across it? On what were its footings set, or who laid its cornerstone-while the morning stars sang together and all the angels shouted for joy?
>
> Job 38:4-7 (NIV)

When I was traveling toward the pinprick of light, after my feeble attempts to use my earth movements to get me closer failed, I understood without a doubt that there was something beyond the earth. I was excited and intrigued at the same time. The recognition of knowing I was about to travel into heaven was an immensely desired and elated feeling. I wanted to go and witness what it looked like and how it felt. Did it have smells or tastes? I was not concerned about meeting people I knew. Just ready and willing to be in God's presence was enough for me. The Bible tries to describe God's presence, but boy, it falls short on its description. The brief time I was traveling in the light, the sense of pure and absolute joy reigned through every cell of my being.

There is no way that God did not design our DNA because it was as if my DNA was singing to God as I was traveling toward the light. This may seem as if it is an exaggeration, but I am confessing the truth to you. Do you remember your last roller coaster ride? As the ride hitches itself to the highest point of the ride, you feel a tug with each inch until you reach the apex. As you traverse the highest point, your body shakes with speed as the momentum and curves grasp you while the car hugs the rails. Each rider accepts a blind trust that the mechanics have performed the ride's safety checks for the day as the ride gathers more speed on the twists or turns. Meanwhile, the passengers' screams are heard all the way around the track. For some of us, we can barely hang on to the rail in front of us or to the shoulder pads on us, locking our bodies into place. We involuntarily scream in the feeling of the moment. Traveling into the light is nothing like that. Roller Coasters are outer body forces pressing on our inner bodies. Going to the light is your inner body vibrating and singing outwardly. You sing from your inner self to the light. In the book of Luke, Jesus teaches us that since God causes everything, it is the nature of everything to sing and praise Him, even the inanimate objects.

> As soon as He was approaching, near the descent of the Mount of Olives, the whole crowd of the disciples began to praise God joyfully with a loud voice for all the miracles which they had seen, shouting: "BLESSED IS THE KING WHO COMES IN THE NAME OF THE LORD; Peace in heaven and glory in the highest!" Some of the Pharisees in the crowd said to Him, "Teacher, rebuke Your disciples." But Jesus answered, "I tell you, if these become silent, the stones will cry out!"
>
> Luke 19:37-40 (NIV)

As I ascended, it was the most natural thing to do: *praise the Most High God.* For me, I was praising through song. I can honestly say it felt the most comfortable for me to praise with singing. As I moved closer to the light and the light began enlarging, I felt my singing was part of all the rejoicing in heaven; it was a feeling of rejoining and accompanying with a song in a collective symphony. Most importantly, it was the most amazing experience I have ever had. Every so often, when this world is beating me up, emotionally or physically, I will reflect back on that moment of ascension and gain extraordinary comfort in knowing that God lives. God lives in a more notable and better place than this earth could ever bring. When we join in with the rest of creation singing for our God, it is a euphoria that can never be replicated here on earth.

The Bible attempts to describe it, but in many ways, our language skills are limiting to the vast gloriousness of our God's heaven. For those of you who are desperate to find the truth of heaven and God because life has implored you to question even the simplest of joys that our God has provided for you, I refer back to the story of the mustard seed. Jesus related this parable: "The kingdom of heaven is like a mustard seed, which a man took and planted in his field. Though it is the smallest of all seeds, yet when it grows, it is the largest of garden plants and becomes a tree, so that the birds come and perch in its branches" (Matthew 13:31-32, NIV). If we retain just a smidgen of hope of God in our hearts, God can work with that! He will send you the Holy Spirit to reveal more and more truths to you. For some, the truths may enter a dream. For others, it may be in a magnificent vista on the plains. For some people, the truth comes in the sounds of your children or grandchildren. God will come to you and manage your sensory perception to get across the information that He desires and requires you to know. Do not be upset if it does not happen overnight. For many of us, revelation of truth takes a lifetime, one piece at a time. A pinprick of light is a world of hope that leads to joy and jubilation. Appreciate knowing the truth in the book of Revelation 7 where it is written:

> All the angels were standing around the throne and around the elders and the four living creatures. They fell down on their faces before the throne and worshiped God saying: "Amen! Praise and

glory and wisdom and thanks and honor and power and strength
be to our God for ever and ever. Amen!

Revelation 7:11-12 (NIV)

If you are apprehensive, I challenge you to recite this passage
of scripture throughout the day for three days straight and then see
what our Lord reveals to your heart. I promise you; it will be worth
the risk you will assume in doing it.

The Heart

"For where your treasure is, there your heart will be also."
Matthew 6:21 (NIV)

In the NIV translation of the Bible, the heart is mentioned 725 times. The condition of your heart remains a weighty topic for God. He will analyze it and see if it is worthy of eternity in heaven. Peter may hold the keys to the pearly gates, but your entrance fee is the condition of your heart.

> People were also bringing babies to Jesus for him to place his hands on them. When the disciples saw this, they rebuked them. But Jesus called the children to him and said, "Let the little children come to me, and do not hinder them, for the kingdom of God belongs to such as these. Truly I tell you, anyone who will not receive the kingdom of God like a little child will never enter it."
>
> Luke 18:15-17 (NIV)

Some people have difficulty understanding this quote. I think they get bewildered as to why children, who still have much to learn about praying, fasting, and scripture reading, receive a preference into the kingdom of God. They are spiritually undeveloped or seasoned as adults. They giggle with delight at the simplest of things. Anyone with a van full of young ladies heading to a birthday party can attest to the noise generated from a gaggle of girls. If girls were not in your family, perhaps a truck loaded down with boys heading to a favorite sporting event will examine the auditory levels of a parent's ears with uproarious laughter at the most mundane or silliest of things. Jesus is explaining to us the importance of accepting God with the overflowing joyful heart of a child. Children do not yet know the ways of the world that would inhibit or cause them to overthink Christian beliefs. They sustain unfettered hope in their hearts because they have yet to experience a correlation between hope and harsh reality. They grasp the words of adults at full value, not challenging their authenticity.

After deciding I was not going to stay in the darkness and realizing time was no longer an issue for me, I became determined to move to the light. But as I noted in my near-death account, I became obsessed with trying to deliver the proper prayer for the situation. I tried the 23rd Psalm and mixed up the wording a bit. I tried the Lord's Prayer and managed that one perfectly with no results. As a Christian, many times I heard a specific prayer is appropriate for such-and-such a situation. How do we work at delivering the prayer "just right" for the situation at hand? My Catholic friends were splendid at reciting prayers, especially the ones they had to say for the Rosary (and I had friends who had to say the Rosary quite a lot). My Baptist friends were unquestionably good at reciting scripture passages. They even had quizzes and competitions to test who could say what scripture passage mistake-free. I was not as good as my Baptist friends in recitation, so I defaulted to my Catholic friends and worked on getting the prayer perfect, hoping the prayer would obtain my ticket to the light.

I kept working at the wording in the darkness until I became exhausted and completely gave up. What was I going to do? I did not know, but I sure was not going to stay where I was. Once again, I tried managing the words of my prayer just perfectly. I defaulted to the Lord's Prayer again, making sure I recited every word correctly, just as I was taught. The Bible tells us Jesus instructed us to pray, saying,

> Our Father who art in Heaven hallowed be thy name, thy kingdom come, thy will be done, as it is in heaven. Give us this day our

daily bread and forgive us our trespasses, as we forgive those who trespass against us. And lead us not into temptation, but deliver us from evil. For thine is the Kingdom, the power, and the glory forever and ever Amen.

Matthew 6:9-13 (NKJV)

This is an incredibly important prayer to say. Many a preacher has dissected this prayer in the pulpit or Sunday School classroom in his/her attempt to teach the congregation exactly why Jesus chose the structure of this prayer. I had prayed it perfectly. I knew I recited it perfectly, so why was I not moving to the light? I finally figured out it was because my heart was not in the prayer. It had become routine memory for me, and I was only thirteen years of age! How quickly the heart can leave the declarations of the faith. At my young age, I already had a serious heart condition.

Fed up about my inability to leave the darkness, I gave up on the syntax of my prayer and resorted to talking to God as if I was talking to my friend. Was it a formal prayer? Nope. Was it in the formal structure of the Lord's Prayer? Nope. Did it contain an honest and raw request? Yup. Transferring the energy of my thoughts from my brain to a feeling of energy emanating from my heart, I said, "God and Jesus, I just want to be with you. I want to go to the light." It was a cry of desperation, composed of a raw request from the center of my being. That was it. No special magical words were in my petition. There was no theological structure to my prayer. It was just a straightforward request from my heart. God examines our hearts more than He overhears our words. Christians need to grasp this because it is critical to our salvation. When we genuinely believe from our hearts that God is our God and Jesus is our Lord, God claims and gathers us as one of His children.

Our God is such a magnificent father that He provided us Jesus, who walked on this earth to redirect humanity to God and His glory. "For God so loved the world that He gave His only begotten son"

(John 3:16, NIV). I realize many of you have heard these words or seen the signs loyal Christians hold up at sporting events. I am not denying how important these words are for the world, but for me, the more considerable emphasis should focus on verses seventeen and eighteen that follow the John 3:16 line of Scripture.

> For God did not send his Son into the world to condemn the world, but to save the world through him. Whoever believes in him is not condemned, but whoever does not believe stands condemned already because they have not believed in the name of God's one and only Son.

John 3:17-18 (NIV)

It was because of God's own heart for man; He came in the human form of Jesus and taught us how to get back to God. All the ways of the world had corrupted man's thinking. The Lord had to remind the great prophet Samuel "...The LORD does not look at the things people look at. People look at the outward appearance, but the LORD looks at the heart" (1 Samuel 16:7, NLT). We have to redirect our thinking to our hearts both in times of strife and in opportunity. The Psalms prompts us to refocus the core of our thinking to God's message in our hearts so that we do not fall victim to the temptations of the world that can do nothing for us. The world only seeks to produce an increase of anxiety, confusion, grief, loneliness, pain, and ill health, just to name a few. The world will give us a heart "attack." When we treasure the Word of God in our hearts, we become battle-ready for the world's trials. "I have hidden your word in my heart that I might not sin against you" (Psalm 119:11, NIV). Jesus did not walk on this earth, telling us this would be an uncomplicated life. He came to tell us it will be a life well-lived if we believe in God and all that He has given to us.

God cherishes a heartfelt relationship with you. Have you had your heart checked lately? I mean, a real heart check where you stand in the rawness of your emotions and talk with God about the good, the bad, and the ugly of your life. Have you identified the mistakes you have made towards family members and others? Have you analyzed the times in your life where you could have been a better person? Have you asked Him why life is unfair to you? Why does it inevitably seem that someone else makes out better or paid more for doing less? Have you humbled yourself to learn about God rather than argue about or with Him? When you begin to ask God serious questions, He will begin to deliver you serious answers in return. Only just remember: you may not like the answer you get. God perceives your condition from a heavenly perspective, not an earthly one. He sees how connected every one of us is to each other, whether we get along with each other or not. Specific people and situations placed in our lives urge us to grow in our spiritual walk. Guess what? It is not a leisurely walk for anyone. Even though we may feel a person enjoys it all (a big house, a nice car, a beautiful family), they experience trials and tribulations just like everyone else, so they may grow in their faith.

St. John of the Cross (Juan de Yepes y Alvarez) wrote a poem entitled "Dark Night," describing the miserable conditions where he was imprisoned as punishment for his attempts to reform the Carmelite order within the church. Chained and tortured in a tiny cell, with no air in the summer and no heat in the winter, St. John never broke down. However, despite his horrific conditions, St. John of the Cross demonstrated for us how to let go of the earthly bonds and focus only on God. His earthly trials challenged his temperament to let go of all things in this world and transport his heart to the glory of our Creator. His poem has had a profound effect on the Christian movement throughout the centuries, many of whom have found themselves in dark prisons and have had a similar faith transformation.[2]

> Into this dark night souls begin to enter when God draws them
> forth from the state of beginners...and begins to set them in the

state of progressives...to the end that, after passing through it, they may arrive at the state of the perfect, which is that of the Divine union of the soul with God.[3]

For God to perform miracles in your life, first, you must believe. We all walk uphill in this earthly life. In the town of Nazareth, two blind men who needed healing approached Jesus. Before Jesus healed them, He first had questioned their belief in Him. The question Jesus asked the men was rather blunt, but it was critically necessary. Why would Jesus relieve the men from their blindness if they did not believe He could do it in the first place? Since Jesus is wholly God and fully human, He could have restored the men no matter what. Hence, the men occupied a critical role in the miracle's fulfillment. A relationship is between two people who agree to interact (or agree to not interact, in some cases). Jesus could heal, but He needed the men who were blind in a committed relationship with Him. It is the blind men's belief in Jesus as the Son of God, who could accomplish miracles that allowed the miracle to heal their blindness.

The question I present to you is whether you are going to take God with you or try to do it alone? The world is a lonely and empty place. To traverse this earth *with* our Creator ushers us to a greater life value. Without relying on scientific theory, check your heart to consider if you sincerely believe in God and His magnificent glory. As a result, you will find a world rich in love. It will be worth it.

The Journey

"in all your ways submit to him, and he will make your paths straight."
Psalm 3:6 (NIV)

My maternal grandfather was born in 1897. He died in 1972, at the age of seventy-five. In his lifetime, the world went from driving a horse and buggy as the principal form of transportation to watching a man walk on the moon in 1969. A master tool-and-die tradesman, he was constantly astonished at the technological progress of civilization in such a short time. Something modern was invented or improved upon at every turn. As an adolescent boy of ten or so, he could no more imagine, let alone describe, what life would be like at the time of his death. To set this into perspective, my grandfather turned ten years old in 1907; it was not until the following year, the Ford Motor company produced the first Model T car in 1908. During his life, the increased use in technology throughout our society was overwhelmingly mystifying.

Let me cite the example of someone who lived in the late 1800s, like my grandfather. The individual travels to the future and rides in a jet plane; he then returns to his own era of the late-19th century and tries to explain to family and friends the jet ride experience. For us, air travel represents a way of life. In fact, we occupy hours on the internet searching for the most competitive flight with the fewest stops and layovers; anything to reduce the travel time. How many times have you endured a delayed and overcrowded flight? To decompress from experience, you discuss in immense detail every little thing that happens to you on the travel to your friends and family. Now try recounting that experience to someone who had never been on a flight. Merely imagining the flight, the interior of the jet, and where the jet went in such a short time would have mind-boggled anyone in the late 1800s. The average person of that time could not synthesize the information to comprehend thoroughly what the time traveler had experienced. Furthermore, the time traveler would have extreme difficulty trying to put the jet flight into late-19th century vocabulary. People would call the time traveler crazy, maybe even put the person in a padded room for his/her own safety. Eventually, because the average person of that era could not relate to a jet travel experience, the story would be ballyhooed, ignored, and even silenced. This is what it is like to tell you of my journey into the light. I am trying to articulate in terms the average 21st-century person would understand for a concept, not of this earth.

Martin Luther, the prominent reformist of the church in the 16th century, recognized it correctly. As a biblical studies teacher at Wittenberg University, Luther welcomed academic discussions about the Christian faith. He struggled with his own sinful nature and acceptance as a righteous man. In 1515, he began studying the book of Romans, which led to his now-famous religious epiphany. "Man is saved only by his faith in the merit of Christ's sacrifice."[4] This is exactly what I experienced as I faced the light of God, the precise moment of life after life. God desires you to believe in Him. When we believe in Him, we begin to draw back the curtains of our lives and allow Him to enter our hearts and minds and be a part of our strength as we traverse the hills and valleys of this journey called life. No matter what we have rendered or not rendered, when we believe in the Lord God, then God can send the Holy Spirit to encourage us with our life path. As we mature in our Christian faith, we go from believing God as an almighty deity in the sky, acting as a grand puppet master, to experiencing the love of a father, Abba God. A God who cares and loves us fully. At the moment we stand in front of Him, we stand there with all of our brokenness, knowing full well that we have believed too little, too late, and done too little, too late. All we retain is our raw inner self, exposing what love we have for Him. God says, "Welcome home, I have been waiting for you."

Having figured out that the key to going to God was my heart's condition and not the words I said, I began to move. (As an aside, I must apologize to all of those who believe the King James Version remains the only authentic version of the Bible. I love the King James Bible and relied on it to practice for my Shakespeare test in my high school British Literature class. I devoted hours reading the Psalms out loud in my bedroom to develop the rhythm of Elizabethan English. Woefully, all the "thees" and "thous" did not assist me moving a millimeter closer to God. It was my love that moved me closer to God.) As I neared the pinprick of light, I began to giggle, not because it was a humorous experience, rather because I was finally moving. Excitedly, escaping the misery of darkness offered me tremendous hope. The thirteen-year-old in me giggled so hard my movement stopped and I had to center my thoughts once again. Like any juvenile learner, I began with the process of repeating the words of prayers and passages, going nowhere, until I realized it was nothing to do with the words of belief but rather the belief itself that propelled me to the light. My heart needed to be focused on my love for God. Once I concentrated on my heart's love for God and asked to go to Him, I resumed my journey to God.

There was no feeling of temperature from the light. That is to say, I did not feel the heat emanating as you would the heat stemming from the sun here on earth. What I did perceive was love. The light was energy, and the energy's name was love. Nothing but pure and perfect love. It is imperative everyone understands this. On earth, we have a periodic table of elements. Many students in school have had to memorize the chart and its organization. Combining the table's elements gives us compounds that possess different properties than the elements in their original absolute state. God is pure love. Love is

His energy. If we enter heaven with anything other than a pure heart of love, we, in essence, change heaven to a compounded existence. God cannot have that in heaven because it does not work with His creation. Heaven must remain pure in love because God is love, and God lives in heaven, where love is in its purest state.

The closer I traveled to the light, the greater the feeling of love and hope I experienced. As the light was surrounding me, I realized the light was Jesus, the Holy Spirit, and God; all three were in the light. Much like white light here on earth refracts into the colors of the rainbow after a rain shower has passed, the divine light contained all three beings into one light. It was a journey of hope. At last, I was leaving the darkness and entering into the light of heaven and the hope of a better world than the void I was leaving.

The light presented a sense of belonging. I knew God was my Creator and the Creator of all things. There was a feeling of being put back together, a reconnecting sensation. I realized the earth was not my origination but rather a place of short-term existence. Happily, rid of earth and its confinement, worries of my family or friends at my departure never entered into the processes of my mind. God absorbs all your thoughts because God is the source of your life. Traveling deeper into the core of the light, it became my very being to begin to sing for the Lord God Almighty. My singing seemed as if it originated from my DNA. Every cell seemed to vibrate in musical rhythm, in concert with angelic voices. It was absolutely amazing. The closer I drew to the light, the stronger my singing became; the more I felt connected to God and the more love I felt.

As I traveled closer to the light, revelations in my mind would awaken my thoughts to a higher level of thinking. To ask me the exact revelation as I traveled in the light remains a challenging question to answer. Many people who have undergone near-death experiences can provide specifics to this. Whereas I remember my mind awakening to God as the Creator, Jesus' formidable mission, and the Holy Spirit as the energy force that traverses the earthly realm. It is critical to understand the Holy Spirit is constantly seeking open hearts while teaching and revealing God to us. God has never abandoned us. The sensation of leaving the micro-ness of earth and reaching into the macro-ness of heaven was evident. Heaven is grander and loftier than we could ever imagine. That is why the Bible is a "tool" for us to use to remain close to God. The earthly terms used in the Bible place limits on the grandeur of God. Even our Jewish friends historically do not spell out Yahweh; preferably, they use the tetragrammaton YHWH. The Jewish believe that once you place all the letters in the name, you have lessened your respect for God and placed limitations on Him.[5] After experiencing the light, I can honestly say this is accurate. Writing this book is relatively difficult for me since I have to describe a heavenly experience in terms that do not exist. Whatever terms I implement to describe my journey to the divine light will always be wholly inadequate.

In my New Testament course, my professor asked the class about our ministries and what translations of the Bible the congregations preferred to read. One student bluntly responded: "Are you kidding me? I am a youth pastor. I am happy if the kids open a Bible, let alone the "right" Bible." That is the way it should be. Read the biblical translation that speaks to your heart and renders you closer to God. God gave us the Bible in numerous translations to help keep Him close to our hearts. Many a Christian has begun his/her walk using the Message Bible, which really is not the Bible, per se. It is a story of the Bible. However, it is a translation of the Bible, written in simple terms, which allowed many to come to know our Lord and Savior, Jesus Christ. As a Christian matures in faith, the favorite translation will change. This is normal for the Christian journey.

> This is the verdict: Light has come into the world, but people loved darkness instead of light because their deeds were evil. Everyone who does evil hates the light, and will not come into the light for fear that their deeds will be exposed. But whoever lives by the

truth comes into the light, so that it may be seen plainly that what they have done has been done in the sight of God.

John 3:19-21 (NIV)

After my return to this earthly state, I have often wondered why anyone would wish their ill grandparent to remain here on earth when the loved one could be living in this pure, divine love light with God. It is an absolute blissful state where there is peace, love, and tranquility. It is insensitive of us to not wish for our senior relatives to pass on to a greater glory; instead pleading for them to linger in feeble-mindedness while attached to a plethora of life-sustaining medications. Now, I am no Dr. Kevorkian with death wishes for our elderly. We all go when God summons us home. However, to pray for your ill grandparent to endure a compromised quality of life after having lived an extensive one is a selfish prayer. That situation is about the earth and earthly self-centered lives. A person is more alive in the light of God than ever could be on earth. Empower them to go! If they love Jesus, release them to go dance with Jesus. Those who lack an understanding of the story of Jesus want to sustain life, no matter how compromised a life. For those of us who have an understanding of Jesus, letting go brings healing and a better life. Furthermore, if we know the pureness of God's love for us, we must inform everyone of God's love for the world and a greater life in eternity. Jesus tells us, "...Let the dead bury their own dead, but you go and proclaim the kingdom of God" (Luke 9:60, NIV).

Our journey with God is about our belief in Him as our great, loving God. It does not matter how long you have walked with God. The key to the light is your heart's belief in God. Jesus tells the parable about the workers in the vineyard in the gospel of Matthew, chapter twenty. The landowner went out seeking laborers to work his vineyard five different times during the day. In the evening, the landowner went to the foreman to gather all the workers from the field. Each worker, no matter how long they had worked in the field, received a denarius, as promised. Jesus tells us this is the promise of heaven. When I was traveling to the light, it did not matter how long I believed in Jesus, just that I believed. This is critical information for our loved ones, friends, neighbors who may worry about their Christian journey duration. Whether it be a mature or new one, God will welcome you if your belief in Jesus is honest and true in your heart.

The Sides

"In the presence of God and of Christ Jesus, who will judge the living and the dead..." 2 Timothy 4:1 (NIV)

Please excuse my vulgarity, but accountability sucks. When we are held responsible for our actions or our leadership in a situation, and the outcome is not a desired one, we bear the emotional weight of failure. The same is true with our lives. Every one of us beyond the age of accountability (between twelve and seventeen, depending on maturity level) is responsible for the good, the bad, and the horribly wrong situations in our lives that result from our decisions. Sometimes, making a less-than-best choice remains the only choice we have to get out of a temporary situation. Subsequently, there are those bad life decisions where we keep ourselves, our family members, and our colleagues in a suspended state of impending ruin, whether it be economic, physical, psychological, or spiritual imprisonment. Sometimes our stacked decisions are so much on top of each other that we find ourselves buried in a mountainous pile of bad life choices. The incredible weight of our choices is so burdensome we are unable to step away from them to clean up our lives. At this point, some of us choose to give up and merely stay in a ruinous state, swimming in our own toilet water. We become too terrified to make another decision that may compound the matter and find ourselves in a cascading, systemic life situation.

Modern wars result from this phenomenon. Political alliances, restraint of trade, and control of resources empower governments and subdue people. One political decision leads to another decision, which leads to another and another. Ultimately, one side becomes so angered at the other, for whatever reason, that land destruction and the slaughter of humankind takes precedence over the cost of the children's innocence. The 2002 action movie *We Were Soldiers,* starring Mel Gibson,[6] jarred a deeply suppressed memory of mine. I had long forgotten about the delivery of death notices by taxi drivers until the movie reminded me.

Living in Fort Monroe, VA, during the 1960s, I would ride my bike down the neighborhood street lined with row after row of cookie-cutter-style government houses. Looking for a specific set of quarters, a taxi driver would stop and ask any kid for directions. All of us were heavily counseled by our parents about what to do when such a taxi approached us. We were to get home immediately and tell our moms. Our moms would run out of the house to intervene with the taxi driver. My mom never allowed us to look out the window of our assigned quarters during those times. We had to find something to do, such as read a book or play a board game, until the message had been properly delivered by a community member. My mom knew the news contained in the telegram would travel fast enough. She did not want us peering into a family's moment of heartbreak at the loss of their soldier.

Even to this day, news always travels swiftly in a military community. Funny how I had forgotten about the taxis delivering death notices until the movie jarred my memory. Instantly, I was back to my life as a seven-and-eight-year-old girl, riding her bike as fast as she could to get home to tell her mom a taxi was in the neighborhood. Such devastating times rip the hearts out of the many affected people. Military families never desire war and yet are willing to give so much of themselves for peace. We know and live with the price of erroneous political decisions.

In her book, *The Hiding Place*, Corrie Ten Boom, describes the destructive invading German forces in Holland during World War II. Initially, the attacks on citizen Jews were minor and infrequent, as the German occupational forces were labeling their neighbors and friends with a yellow star on their clothing. As the invasion grew, the systemic, devastating ethnic cleansing of Dutch Jewish people prevailed. The Ten Boom family had to look microscopically at their Christian faith in this time of horror and consciously decide how a Christian should behave. Not all programs to support were ethical. In its attempt to save the persecuted Jews, the Dutch underground system was peppered with "...stealing, lying, and murder. Was this what God wanted in times like these? How should a Christian act when evil was in power?"[7] At what cost is our faith? What is faith in a time of crisis?

We are all faced with challenges, no matter who we are or where we live. Depending on economic and political stressors, sometimes we are confronted with unbelievably and incredibly complex decisions, just like Corrie Ten Boom. We are confronted with executing life-altering decisions: whether it be about a new job, a business, a relationship, disciplining a child, handling the death of a loved one, etc. We all have weighted choices to make in our lives. We must learn how to decide on the next best step in our lives, even in the midst of political upheavals and economic strife. Every so often, that step does not get us to our desired outcome, but it does move us out of our current situation. Time and again, we need practice learning how to take the next best step.

Furthermore, we are responsible for only the decisions in our own lives, not those of our parents or grandparents. God exclusively looks at our thought processes and the decisions we made as we stand in front of Him. God recognizes all the steps it involved for you to carry out each and every one of those choices as well. He knows if you make choices through anger, confusion, hurt, loneliness, love, or obedience. He is also profoundly understanding of the cascading and compiling effect of our decisions in our lives. He is acutely aware of the effects of your parents' decisions on your life as well. Moreover, God does not hold us responsible for our children's decisions once they are past the age of accountability. Many parents want to bear the emotional burden of their adult children's ill-fated decisions, but that is not how the program works. Each adult is responsible for his or her own choices.

> But you may ask, "Why doesn't the son suffer punishment for the father's iniquity?" Since the son has done what is just and right, carefully observing all My statutes, he will certainly live. The person who sins is the one who will die. A son won't suffer punishment for the father's iniquity, and a father won't suffer punishment for the son's iniquity. The righteousness of the righteous person will be on him, and the wickedness of the wicked person will be on him.

Ezekiel 18:19-20 (HCSB)

Our mighty God appreciates and desires us to live in communal love and concern for others. We are fostered for a relationship with fellow humankind, as well as a relationship with our God. Therefore, we must prefer a life of love and concern for others, even though we may not enjoy such an understanding. Our God is a God of love and empathy, whose mercies are new every day. He desires each of us to renew and reorient ourselves daily in a better life with Him.

Here is the catch: using God's guidance, we must methodically and purposefully choose to invest in the soundest decision we can with the information we secure at that specific moment in time. Many of us have abandoned the idea of God and His ability to encourage us when we require it most. People have turned to abuse, alcohol, drugs, extramarital affairs, overspending, self-pity, just to name a few, in their quest to gratify their own needs. These "solutions" only create a deeper set of problems. The world's answers do not resolve life's problems. They never have and never will. They succeed only in causing more chaos in their lives. When we focus on God aiding us rather than us helping ourselves, our next best step coaxes us to a better place than we were beforehand.

As for you, if you redirect your heart and lift up your hands to Him in prayer-if there is iniquity in your hand, remove it, and don't allow injustice to dwell in your tents—then you will hold your head high, free from fault. You will be firmly established and unafraid. For you will forget your suffering, recalling it only as waters that have flowed by. Your life will be brighter than noonday; its darkness will be like the morning. You will be confident, because there is hope. You will look carefully about and lie down in safety.

Job 11:14-18 (HCSB)

God is profoundly aware many of us do not come from great home environments. I am certain He wishes we did. Nonetheless, He recognizes the conditions in which you were raised. He recognizes all the decisions your parents made, whether they were worthy or destructive while you were under their care, no matter how long that was. Your parents have to face God for their successes and failures, just as you do. God is here to haul you out of the vast wasteland of emotional pain that man creates for himself. Allow God to encourage you to make better decisions.

Undertake your journey through prayer. Just talk to God, using your own voice, inside of you or out loud. Talk to God about yourself, your family, your boss, your children, the driver in front of you on the road. Any subject you choose will work, but it has to commence with you talking to God. Do not worry about the precise wording. Begin asking for guidance in your situation, the one that is bothering you the most.

I was a volunteer prayer guide at my local church. My task was to stand silently against the wall in the sanctuary, waiting for an individual to come to me and listen to the concerns. After a few moments of the person telling me the situation, I would stand with them and privately pray for the person and the circumstances. One Sunday, a beautiful young woman who I had never seen before waited for a lull in the line of people before coming up for prayer. I think she was trying to figure this church thing out. After I had stood there alone for a moment, she sprung up from the pew and quickly walked toward me. I clasped her hand, as was my established habit, and inquired as to how I could assist her. With desperation in her voice, she asked me, "How do I talk to Jesus? I do not know how." I kind of chuckled and said, "You talk to Jesus just like you are talking to me now. You already have the mechanics, just direct the questions to God and Jesus. Just talk." She asked, "Out loud?" I replied wholeheartedly, "Yes." I mentally prepared to pray with her to offer her strength to talk to God when she abruptly turned away from me and returned to the pew. I have not seen her since that day, but it is my sincerest hope and prayer she began talking to God and has never ceased.

Once you get that sixth-sense feeling after your prayer, then begin to act on it. Sometimes it takes only a moment to gain that sense; sometimes it takes a considerable endurance. For some of us who are mature Christians, we know that some prayers take a long time for an answer. Nonetheless, Christians know all answered prayers come in God's time and in God's own way. We are only required to sustain the relationship from our end. God is always maintaining the relationship from His end. Remember, beginning to pray requires you to move one step at a time. Use your implicit trust to pray to God and then rely on that feeling or sixth sense you get in return. Consequently, your belief in Him will grow.

Be aware that once you embark on your journey with God, your family and friends may become hyper-critical of you. You must stay focused on how *you* are going to improve *your* life and be firm in rejecting the voices of mockery. Being a Christian is not easy against today's backdrop. Then again, it was not for the first-century Christians either. Rome burned while emperor Nero blamed all the Christians living there for the vast carnage. Twenty-first-century Christians are just the latest in joining the group.

Once you start to rely on God to impart to you the internal knowledge for your next best step, then begin to read the Bible—

any Bible. It is from the Bible that we learn about so many of the successes and failures of the people who have lived before us. Your situation is not unique to you. Someone in the Biblical narrative has gone through exactly the same thing you are going through. It is a wonderful book that can guide us in all things because all the answers are there hidden in the lives of the biblical people. This beautiful historical divinely inspired document retells what the faithful has done, or not done, and how God intervened in their lives. God desperately wants a relationship with all of His children.

As you begin to routinely read the Bible, an understanding of sin and its effects on our lives can be identified. Sin is the falling away from God and not using His guidance for your life. God knows we are victims of the world at large and that *every one* of us will step away from His narrow path. If we redirect ourselves to His ways and right our course, then we will grow intimately closer to God.

Sad to relate, the church bears a social black eye from pointing fingers and condemning others outside the church who are not Christian-minded. The problem, I believe, is that most people today are not raised with any religion. Worst, they believe everyone's truth is a truth and therefore do not know right from wrong. I am absolutely confident that praying to Jesus is the first "best step" in anyone's life. Faithful Christians choose Christ not because they feel they are worthier than everyone else; rather, the world is so tempting, we need Christ to keep placing us back on God's path. Authentic Christians recall just how many times they have resorted to being just like the world—regretfully having done horribly destructive and wrong things. True Christians know they are not perfect. Only Christ is.

Once you begin to understand that the biblical people centuries before you have had the same life issues as you, an opening up of the mind and heart ensues. You connect with Biblical events on an emotional level. Belief in Jesus as part of the triune God becomes foundational in your heart. It is from that connection, known only to you and God, that you can decide to transform your life for good. This is recognized as repentance. The key to repentance is to realize the error of your ways, ask for forgiveness, *then do not do it anymore.* Modern-day Christians understand praying, reading the Word, and seeking forgiveness. Unfortunately, they are severely lacking in removing the unacceptable behavior from their lives. They go to church on Sunday and are back to the ways of the world on Monday. They demand God to justify their actions rather than sanctify their lives.

Non-Christians look at this absurd cycle of "good on Sunday, bad on Monday" and think Christians are just as phony as the latest Hollywood horror movie. A true Christian wears the heart of Christ—not because a believer feels more superior than anyone, but because a firm believer's reliance on Jesus is so strong, one wants to represent the life of Christ. As a fair warning to those who profess Jesus Christ as their Lord and Savior but neglect to modify their behavior, they will be held accountable at a higher level than those who barely knew Jesus.

> Not everyone who says to me, "Lord, Lord," will enter the kingdom of heaven, but only the one who does the will of my Father who is in heaven. Many will say to me on that day, "Lord, Lord, did we not prophesy in your name and in your name drive out demons and in your name perform many miracles?" Then I will tell them plainly, "I never knew you. Away from me, you evildoers!"
>
> Matthew 7:21-23 (HCSB)

This never-ending cycle of repeating egregious behavior will present a problem for those Christians who violate the repentance step when they encounter God in their death. You must abandon what you are doing wrong and allow the Holy Spirit to steer you to the appropriate way of life. Jesus tells of the parable of the lost coin in Luke 15:8-10 when He teaches about how important it is to change your ways.

Or what woman who has ten silver coins, if she loses one coin, does not light a lamp, sweep the house, and search carefully until she finds it? When she finds it, she calls her woman friends and neighbors together, saying, "Rejoice with me, because I have found the silver coin I lost!" I tell you, in the same way, there is joy in the presence of God's angels over one sinner who repents.

Luke 15:8-10 (HCSB)

The angels will rejoice over just one person who chooses to live a life more devoted to God. The more a person repents from life's ill-considered decisions, the more Christ-like the person will become. The love for Jesus will grow deeper into the heart, and it will begin to become second nature to carry out the will of God. "The perfect life" will not happen, but it will be better. A perfect life can exclusively be obtained in heaven with our Creator God. Jesus did not promise us a life without trials; rather, He promised us as followers a life that would be a *worthwhile* one.

When the light was about ten feet in diameter, and my body was fully enveloped with God's precious glory and love, I was yanked to the right. Finding myself in a grand space and overwhelmingly disappointed in my curtailed heavenly trip, I promptly began questioning God as to why. In the distance, the elderly gentleman slowly walked to me as I began getting a feel of the vastness of this immense space. Not nearly as dark as the first void and disappointingly out of the true light, I realized another "test" was about to unfold.

In my insistence to return to the light of God, I was acutely aware of how I was maneuvered to the right of the light. It was an involuntary vigorous pull by an unseen force to the right side of the light vortex. To my heavenly elder, I gestured with my left hand God's last known position as I demanded to carry out my journey to heaven's final destination. Directionally, if I was pointing to the left side as the point of reentry to God's light, then I was presently standing in the right side. Not happy with my delayed arrival to the heavenly kingdom, I instinctively knew I was protected where I was and that no harm would come to me. Otherwise, I would have tried to defend myself from this gentleman and remove myself from the surroundings, whether it was possible for me to do so or not. I intuitively knew that with this elderly gentleman, I was secure to forcefully proclaim my heartfelt desire to return to God's tracker beam of light. In other words, it was safe for me to have a "hissy fit" in front of him without fear of harm.

If I felt safe and secure to the right, then by default in reasoning (which could be wrong), the left would be unsafe. What was to the left of the light? I do not know. I do not think I want to know, either. I must defer to the Bible and what the Word warns us about in the last days. Matthew 25:31-34 explains that Jesus will come back and sit on his throne and sort the people.

> When the Son of Man comes in His glory, and all the angels with Him, then He will sit on the throne of His glory. All the nations will be gathered before Him and He will separate them one from another, just as a shepherd separates the sheep from the goats. He will put the sheep on His right and the goats on the left. Then the King will say to those on His right, 'come, you who are blessed by My Father, inherit the kingdom prepared for you from the foundation of the world...
>
> Matthew 25:31-34 (HCSB)

Therefore, I must urgently warn there is a left and right side once we leave this earthly realm. There is only one truth in God's heavenly dimension. We cannot fast-talk our way to the side of our choosing. God chooses. He chooses based on our hearts here on earth. Please, I am imploring you to understand the finality of the situation. If you do not choose God with your heart here on earth, it will be a catastrophic failure for your eternal soul.

God will place you either to His right or to His left. This is not a game where you get to practice your slick negotiating skills.

God looks at your heart. It is either right or left, in or out, with or without. Unlike me, most people do not receive a second chance by coming back and try to do better with their lives. For most people who traverse from the earth to the other side, the decision is final. It is terminal for all of time, never-ceasing. Choose your life decisions wisely in this world so you get to rest in the light of our Triune God forever. Life with God is a real existence. Jesus is real. Make great choices now, so you will not regret them later. Jesus promises us a life with God if we choose Him here on this earth.

The Return

"A man's steps are directed by the Lord, How then can anyone understand his own way?" Proverbs 20:24 (NIV)

God is the Creator of *all* things. Nothing organic in this world is haphazardly created, not even you—no matter the mindset or location of your biological parents when they produced you. How do we know this? It is simple, look at everyone. Everyone's eyes are in the same place: their nose, their mouth, their ears; all of us support the identical design. My ears are not where my ankles should be. Your nose is not in the middle of your back. There is an order to creation. There is an order to your creation. You were created with specificity in mind. A righteous God specifically places all of the good things in you. In fact, God had designed you before you were placed on this earth. You are part of an elaborate team, and God selected you to be on His team. God produced man in His image. You are not a mistake. Your mistakes are not the total sum of who you are. The God who breathed everything into existence, to include the mountains and seas, created every part of your DNA for a specific purpose. You are not the product of a chaotic tumble of evolution. The world and everything in it is a specifically and uniquely designed picture, and you are a significant piece of that entire picture.

Have you put a puzzle together only to have one piece missing? As you view the puzzle in its entirety, enjoying the fruits of your labor and the beauty of the puzzle, your eye keeps gravitating to the empty spot. For the majority of us, having that missing piece would be a frustrating vacancy. That is how the world would be without you in it. You are significant, no matter what anyone says or writes about you. You are so special to God that He put food on the earth to feed you, birds to sing to you, the sun to shine on you, the smell of fresh air to relax you, and beautiful vistas to enrich you. God made you out of love because His elemental essence is nothing but love. Anything less of a notion of God's love for you remains merely a fragment of the original source of love. "...Even as he chose us in him before the foundation of the world, that we should be holy and blameless before him. In love he predestined us..." (Ephesians 1:4-5, ESV). God elected you *before* the foundation of the world and then created a world in which to live. The Lord reveals to Jeremiah, "for I know the plans I have for you, declares the LORD, plans for welfare and not for evil, to give you a future and a hope" (Jeremiah 29:11, ESV). The prophet Jeremiah confirms God has a grander plan for each of us, as well as all believers. We are of divine design, for a greater good. "Your eyes saw me when I was formless; all my days were written in Your book and planned before a single one of them began" (Psalms 139:16, HCSB). You are so important to God that He wrote about you in His book before your formation in your mother's womb. That makes you very special, indeed.

So here is the question that many might be asking; if we are so special to God, then why is life so hard? Excellent question. At thirteen, I already knew how hard life could be from my parents' experience with the US Army, friends, and the economic strife on the streets of Indonesia, to name a few. Some of you have lived in homes that were abusive, alcohol and drug-filled, maybe economically depressed, all of which are peppered with emotional and physical suffering. Clearly, life is toilsome.

I loudly professed my desire to remain with God during my near-death experience, but that was not to be. I was commanded, "there was more for me to do." Life would have been so much easier if my "heavenly elder" had described to me exactly what that was. Just tell me what I need to do, I will do it, and then everything will be peachy. The problem was my heart's condition would not have continued to mature. I would have devoted my life to following a "to-do" list rather than searching my heart for what I felt was right and following it. We are not puppets on God's string. We have free will to choose in this life. God desires us to choose Him, but He is not going to force us to choose Him.

I enjoy swimming for exercise and frequent my local indoor pool on the military installation near where I live. As a lap swimmer, I have to wait for the scuba class using the pool before lap swim to complete their scheduled lessons. As the scuba students entered the locker rooms, those of us preparing for our swim would enjoy polite small talk with them. For a short time, the mainly male-dominated scuba class gained a female student. At the close of her daily class session, I would always inquire about her training. She would respond with, "it was good" or "okay." One day I asked her why she was in the class, and I will never forget what she told me. She had been a recreational scuba diver for many years and enjoyed it. Wanting to scuba full-time as a profession, she opted to enter the military because the money was more substantial than in the civilian world. The soldier was able to combine her love of scuba diving with a paycheck. With her diving expertise as a civilian, the Army training was reasonably simple for her. How perfect is that?!

My husband is a phenomenal car mechanic, especially with older vehicles. He enjoys the process of problem-solving while working on our family vehicles. After three years in the Army, my husband attended college and earned his first degree in Automotive Mechanics. After graduation, his first job was at a local gas station, maintaining and repairing cars, which was exactly what he desired, or so he thought. After about six months of working under someone else's management, he realized he liked working on cars as a hobby rather than as a job. For him, it was the creative process of figuring out a problem that gave him the joy of working on cars. When he worked on a customer's vehicle, it was merely completing a "to-do" list created by someone else. His heart was not into the job. He eventually quit and went back into the Army, where he had far more career successes in the medical field than he would have had if he had stayed working as a mechanic. Going back into the Army allowed him to renew his joy of working on his cars.

The life lessons of these two examples show if you can find a hobby that pays the bills, great! Otherwise, find a job that pays for the hobby—a legal hobby. More importantly, God uniquely creates us with specific interests for a reason. Each of us is exceptionally designed for His needs. Each person comprises of likes, dislikes, and talents of all types, which is a part of the greater God team. God always implements your expertise in whatever you love to do into His plan. Part of our life lesson is figuring out the Godly gifts with which we have been blessed. You have to get to know the Godly created "unique you."

Many of us feel saddled with burdensome career and life choices. We struggle emotionally, financially, mentally, physically, and even socially. We have a longing in our hearts to somehow correct our lives, to prevent the pain of our distress. On the odd occasion, life throws us some terribly bad curveballs, and we have to adjust and overcome them. How do we do that? How do we execute a life-changing decision when a situation is forced upon us?

In 1987, I was laid off from my job. The loss of employment lunched me into an emotional tailspin. I examined everything about myself, including my self-worth. Without hesitation, I canceled all my plans to attend my high school class reunion that summer. Conservation of finances was of utmost priority. My bills did not stop just because of a corporate buyout. Suddenly, I had to make a significant adjustment to my life. With much deliberation and many nights crying a flood of tears into my bed pillow, I choose to go back to school and obtain my teaching certificate. To this day, I can honestly claim that this heart-wrenching decision was one of the most competent ones I have made.

Like many people, I thoroughly enjoy reading the story of Ruth in the Bible. It is a beautifully written short book in the Old Testament that reveals to us one woman's choice to be a part of God's chosen people. There are various ways one can analyze the book of Ruth, but for the purposes of this writing, I want to concentrate on the critical point where Ruth has to make a significant choice about her life.

Ruth was Naomi's daughter-in-law and a Moabite woman. When Naomi's husband and two sons died, she had to decide what she was planning to do with the rest of her life. Tragedy had stricken her to the core. Ancient Middle Eastern women were dependent on men to live. (Dare I say it is even the case for some women today?) When a husband died, a woman had to rely on another male family member somewhere on the family tree for her life's necessities. In contrast to the Middle East customs in that day, the Israelite women could rightfully own land. In the book of Numbers, the daughters of Zelophehad petitioned Moses for ownership of their father's property, and the Lord, through Moses, granted it to them (Numbers 27:1-8, NIV). This land ownership by non-royal women was a practice directed by God and unique to the Israelites. Our God is different from all the other gods. He identifies women as having value. God always has, and He always will. Despite land ownership, the patriarchal duties of family men are not dismissed when taking care of the women.

The widow Naomi decided to return to her home since the famine that had driven her family away from Bethlehem was long over. Since she was relieved of the social custom of caring for her two widowed daughters-in-law, Orpah and Ruth, Naomi instructs them to return to their respective mothers for living assistance. Orpah returns to her hometown. Whereas, Ruth decides life is worthier with Naomi in the land of Judah, alongside her mother-in-law's Israelite family. She chooses to live with the people who worship Yahweh instead of returning to Moab. This is a significant choice by Ruth. She does not have a male family member in Bethlehem to take care of her upon her arrival, as Naomi does. Nevertheless, Ruth chooses to relocate to Bethlehem with her former mother-in-law. The hope of a better quality of life had to have been far greater than the prospects of her current situation for her to pursue this life-altering decision.

As the biblical story continues, Ruth can collect leftover barley for her and Naomi on Naomi's family farmland after each day's harvest. Since they had no immediate male family members to tend the fields, it became Ruth's responsibility to collect daily provisions. Naomi's distant relative Boaz encouraged Ruth to join the harvesters and allowed her to eat when the harvesters took breaks. When Ruth resumed picking up grain, Boaz ordered his men not to ridicule her. In fact, he ordered them to pull out a few harvested stalks and discard them for her to gather. Ultimately, Boaz fell in love with Ruth at Naomi's meddling encouragement. Wonderfully, as the Gospels of Matthew and Luke portray for us in Jesus' genealogy, it is Ruth who becomes the great-grandmother of the mighty King David.

The book of Ruth is a captivating story in which a young widow had to make a choice about the rest of her life. She could have gone back to her family, reclaimed worshipping their gods, and lived a life with all the customs and practices she knew as a girl. Instead, Ruth chooses to move to a foreign land even though she was a widow without any type of male provider. Customarily, Ruth should have returned to her family in Moab. Yet, she had chosen a life with God's people over her own and had become grafted into God's family tree. Not knowing what to expect, she figured there was something better waiting for her in Bethlehem than what she could find in her childhood home. She followed her heart to God. It is only through the heart's condition that we make decisions that have power and might behind them. Naomi told Ruth not to go Bethlehem. In fact, Naomi instructed her to go home. Contrary to all councils and customs, Ruth's heart decided to be a part of God's people. Against all odds, she regarded it as a more desirable life.

What does your journey look like? What decisions have you made with your whole heart that were completely obtuse to your ordinary way of life? Maybe your life is nothing but a "to-do" list, just ticking off the boxes on the bucket list. God delivers us opportunities to have heart equity in living a life with Him. Why? Because our lives will have more meaning to us. We will have a vested interest in being a part of God's life. Otherwise, life becomes like a dull and boring homework assignment, just doing it to get it done. When we choose to live as a Christian, we enjoy a life knowing that a supreme God, who has exclusively created us for His purpose, will always bless and shelter us.

> Therefore, prepare your minds for action, keep sober *in spirit*, fix your hope completely on the grace to be brought to you at the revelation of Jesus Christ. As obedient children, do not be conformed to the former lusts *which were yours* in your ignorance, but like the Holy One who called you, be holy yourselves also in all *your* behavior; because it is written, 'YOU SHALL BE HOLY, FOR I AM HOLY.'

> 1 Peter 1:13-16 (NASB)

For those of you who question, "if God is so good, then why does evil exist in the world?" "Why should I follow God when the world around me indicates otherwise?" In contrast to God, evil is the absence of love. Is there evil in the world? Yes. Evil is a choice consciously made by a person or entity not to include God. Focus is then directed on the lack of love in the world. The more the devil can twist you away from your relationship with God, the more evil wins. Spoiler alert: evil loses in the end, and love wins. So many people are preferring the side of evil, unaware of the consequences and the decision's finality. Yet, there is hope. When you choose God to direct your life, you are a part of the winning end-time team. Woohoo!

There is an irrationality to evil. Evil can penetrate all aspects of our lives. It seems as soon as there is a cracked door, evil forces gain entry. Evil identifies as many names: abuse, destruction, lies, sickness, violence, and the list goes on. All of us have been victims of evil. Conceivably you are wondering if God is so good and powerful, then why does He choose to allow evil to remain? God should use His powerful, all-knowingness to maintain good in this world and eradicate all evil. Why has not God made a utopia for us if He is such a good God? Ah, that would mean everything would be handed to us on a silver platter. We would have nothing to do but sit on a lido deck lounge chair, demanding service. Where would compassion be if all were right with the world? Possibly you are thinking there would be no need for compassion if everything was satisfactory in the world. That situation begs for another question. If all was good and right, would we need a thinking brain or a feeling heart? God created us to think and feel for a reason. He desires us to engage our thoughts and our emotions in the world and force a decision.

As mentioned, we are not puppets and God is not a puppet master. Made in His image, we are capable to create, design, and work in this world. "Then God said, 'Let Us make man in Our Image, according to Our likeness...'" (Genesis 1:26, HCSB). The Triune God (God, Jesus, and the Holy Spirit) placed Adam and Eve in the Garden of Eden, where God talked and walked with them. Their commonplace lives were bustling with the tasks of maintaining a perfect garden.

When confronted with the tree of knowledge, enticed by the serpent's coaxing, Eve had to make a choice. Genesis 2:16-17 (NIV) states God's directive to Adam (which extends to Eve after her creation) "And the LORD God commanded the man, 'You are free to eat from any tree in the garden; but you must not eat from the tree of the knowledge of good and evil, for when you eat from it you will certainly die.'" Notice the phrasing the NIV translation uses. "For when," meaning God designed Adam and Eve with the ability to choose even though they lived in a perfect garden. Even when Eve handed Adam the apple, Adam had a choice. Adam could have said no to Eve's choice of snack. When they both ate from the apple, then their eyes became opened. All of humanity, male and female, choose to fall away from God. In the paradise of the garden, God tested humanity's heart. By using our hearts, rather than our brains, to carry out our decisions, we enter an authentic and trusting relationship with God. God could have designed us to love Him without requiring any decision-making process, but would that be true love? No. Humanity would be merely ordered minions predesigned to love Him. Authentic love cannot be forced on someone.

Why does God allow the suffering of our loved ones? Well, what would inspire you to create and design if everything was perfect? Humans were created to work. Genesis 1:15 (HCSB): "The Lord God took the man and placed him in the Garden of Eden to work it and watch over it." Yet in paradise, Adam and Eve still had to work. They had to interact with the world around them and commit to decisions about how to care for it.

Regrettably, humans can grow to laziness quite quickly. For example, when my eldest child was three and four years old, her dad and I had to constantly tie her shoes. We would check her shoes for untied laces just before we would let her run and play. Once she reached about four and a half to five years, we repeatedly taught her how to tie her own shoes. In the course of time, after we knew she could successfully tie her shoes, we would advise her, "Tie your shoes. If you don't, you will fall." Like any normal kid, she was too lazy to tie her shoes. She fell a couple of times before she caught on to the idea that she needed to check her own shoes to prevent tripping. She had to consciously set her thoughts to decide safety over pain. So, too, we have to consciously set our minds to the goodness of God to alleviate the pain of evil. For the record, when my youngest child came into our lives, we chose shoes with Velcro ties. Clearly, someone was just as tired of yelling at kids as we were and cared enough to designed Velcro closures to eradicate the problem. Ingenious! This indeed proves the point; our created minds are to do work, but our created hearts are to love.

The choices we select with our minds frequently sway us into trouble. God gives us compassion, so we begin to think with our hearts and choose differently. Suffering provokes us to engage with God to help resolve the problem and develop compassion for others. If teaching us empathy was a true and false question, we would never develop empathy for anyone. By choice, God designed empathy and suffering as essay questions, demanding full answers that are pages long, acutely describing our plucked heartstrings from a deep, emotional well. The condition of the heart is the greatest teacher of all. Evil is a matter of humanity not committing the heartfelt decision to follow God's way for our lives, families, communities, and nations. Otherwise, evil would deliver no sting.

> Today I am giving you a choice of two ways. And I ask heaven and earth to be witnesses of your choice. You can choose life or death. The first choice will bring a blessing. The other choice will bring a curse. So choose life! Then you and your children will live. You must love the LORD your God and obey him. Never leave him, because he is your life...
>
> Deuteronomy 30:19-20 (ERV)

When we choose God and not evil, we lie in His holy hands for protection. Belief in God does not grant a perfect life. Each of us must work daily on our relationship with our Father. God's love for you is reciprocated through your love for Him. He perceives exactly what you require, when you need it and not a moment before. Our lives begin reflecting God's love to our family and friends because Godly love is an absolute and generous love. We choose to behave as if a supreme God embraces us. Chapter three in Colossians describes in detail how we are to behave when we choose to love.

> God has chosen you and made you his holy people. He loves you. So your new life should be like this: Show mercy to others. Be kind, humble, gentle, and patient. Don't be angry with each other, but forgive each other. If you feel someone has wronged you, forgive them. Forgive others because the Lord forgave you. Together with these things, the most important part of your new life is to love each other. Love is what holds everything together in perfect unity. Let the peace that Christ gives control your thinking. It is for peace that you were chosen to be together in one body. And always be thankful.
>
> Colossian 3:12-15 (ERV)

Sad to relate, there will invariably be people who will choose evil over God, for whatever reason. It is *your* responsibility to reflect the love you have discovered in God. Ultimately, it is you and your heart that stand before God on judgment day. Allow no fear. Your adversaries will be responsible for their actions as well. No one escapes judgment. If the people around you consistently choose to avoid God, you possess the right to face that evil and call it out for what it is. Afterward, move on with your life, concentrating on the things God desires you to do. You are to continue on the journey God created solely for you, using all the interests and talents God placed in you.

Be confident and tolerate no fear; God will place His opponents in positions where they will cry out to Him for help. God is an all-knowing being and knows what He is doing. He knows exactly how to gain a person's attention. Ever notice, in a time of true crisis, even the atheist yells for God? Have you watched the videos of people in a local convenience store huddled inside a heavy-door freezer as a tornado approached? In the freezer, the Christians focused on praying away the impending disaster, while the atheists are screaming for Jesus. Funny how they do not want the accountability of Christianity in their daily lives, but the moment their life is in danger, they demand Jesus to protect them. For the record, ever notice there is no anti-Buddha, anti-Mohammed, only an anti-Christ. It is telling as to where the true opposition lies. How can God not exist when people who do not believe in Him cry out to Him?

When you choose God with your heart, God declares you His. It is a beautiful place. "Oh, the depth of the riches of the wisdom and knowledge of God! How unsearchable his judgments, and his paths beyond tracing out!" (Romans 11:33, NIV)

The Final Exam

"Test yourselves to see if you are in the faith. Examine yourselves. Or do you yourselves not recognize that Jesus Christ is in you?—unless you fail the test." 2 Corinthians 13:5 (HCSB)

I have some exceedingly bad news for all of us. There will be a final exam at the end of our lives. With our examined hearts, God judges to see if we can answer two questions. Now, I have some really good news. I am going to tell you what those two questions will be. Yes, I am going to give you the questions before you actually take the test. Why? Because I want you to pass; more importantly, so does God. Remember, I flunked the test and had to come back to earth. However, because I flunked, I gained the privilege to encourage you to pass the test.

In Genesis 4, Adam and Eve's sons, Cain and Abel, presented gifts to God to thank Him for all that He had done for them. Abel did very well, whereas Cain encountered a little difficulty with the assignment. Abel, who was what we would consider a rancher nowadays, raised animals. He offered the best of his livestock's first generation to God. Cain was a farmer who worked the land and grew crops. Cain decided to offer some of the crops to God. The problem with Cain's offering was that it was from neither the best nor the first yield of his harvest, like Abel's. Cain's "you get what you get" gift to God displeased God since God had produced everything for Cain's crop in the first place. God thought Cain could have done better with his offering. Cain became enraged with God. He could not take his anger out on God; it would have been a losing battle. Consequently, Cain took his anger out on his brother Abel and killed him. It is telling all of humanity is descended from a dysfunctional first family.

One of the American hospitality customs my mother taught me was to never go to a person's house empty-handed. If someone is kind enough to grace you with hospitality within the home, then in kind, you should present the homeowner with some little gift of gratitude. Maybe a bag of coffee with a unique flavoring, a bouquet of flowers, or perhaps a novelty gift of some sort. In contrast, many countries around the world practice the custom in reverse. If a person invites someone into the home, the homeowner would offer the guest a bite of food and a drink, or maybe a gift. To refuse this hospitality would be considered an insult. Historically, in homes around the world where famine, drought, or economic distress have affected the country, food and drink are a precious commodity. To refuse to partake in the host's served refreshment is extremely offensive since many times the offered food is at a personal expense, even perhaps offered at the sacrifice of the family's limited food supply.

I remember when we would visit homes in Indonesia; my mom would lecture us just before we stepped inside the house about how we were to eat everything placed before us. Whether it was chocolate-covered grasshoppers or not, we were going to eat it, smile as we ate it, and then say "thank you"! Each of us would have to audibly confess, yes, indeed, we would eat and drink anything offered. Naturally, every home we entered was overwhelmingly gracious with hospitality. Thank goodness we were never served anything like grasshoppers. Customarily, it was some type of cookie, fruit, hot tea, or a soda drink, any and all of which my brothers and I would readily consume to our stomachs' content. The point is, people around the world present gifts to one another in acts of kindness.

All of us possess gifts, and we are tested with those provided gifts to others and God. Here on earth, Jesus demonstrated to us what we are to: feed the hungry, clothe the poor, heal the sick, cast out demons, love God, and love one another. Most importantly, we are to grant this freely and with a heart of kindness. We are not to exploit a person's downtrodden existence using food, water, and medicine as a form of control. However, people cannot be idle and fail to take care of themselves when they are capable of doing so, either. We are to uplift people up in life, willingly bestowing gifts, so others do not need to rely on handouts. There is a distinct difference between the two gifts: the gift of kindness and the gift of manipulation. Woe to those individuals who manipulate food, water, and medicine to suffering people for their own gain.

Our heart becomes strengthened when we provide gifts to others. When we give in the name of Jesus, we encourage the hearts of others. I have mentioned this heart condition so many times. It is what we will present to the Almighty God as our gift back to Him. Importantly, it is not the gifts themselves nor the act of gift-giving that propels us into heaven. However, as the heart condition develops through faith in Christ, we grasp the importance of gift-giving. As Christians, we accept an extremely important job. Engaged in the Great Commission, we are to carry out the message of Jesus Christ. The gospel of Matthew instructs: "So go and make followers of all people in the world. Baptize them in the name of the Father and the Son and the Holy Spirit. Teach them to obey everything that I have told you to do..." (Matthew 28:19-20, ERV)

As you stand in your primary essence before God, you have only your heart to bring, containing all the feelings and thoughts you have felt as you lived your life on earth. Beware, it is a cumulative test! The test will include the period from the day you were accountable to the day you departed from earth, no matter how long or short that time might be.

Having returned from the dark void, I can truthfully tell you the test is *not* a frightening experience; at least, it was not so for me. It is, however, extremely humbling, standing in God's presence, all your thoughts and feelings exposed. Every feeling and thought you have ever had collectively stands before God. In fact, it is what a person presents to God as a personal gift to Him. Our heart is our "hospitality gift" to God when we come before Him in heaven. When I was in the light, the only thing I owned was my life's thoughts and feelings. A person cannot circumvent the test, nor can one's genuine feelings be avoided. Everything is laid out before God. It is the "energy package" you present to Him.

Now, about the test questions themselves. The first question you will have to answer is, who do you say is Jesus Christ? For me, since I called out to God in the darkness and instantly realized the light was the Triune God—God the Father, God the Son, God the Holy Spirit-fused into one beautiful, inviting light, my heart just continued to open up to divine love as I traveled closer. It was a time of confirmation of my belief in Jesus and the magnificence of God. It validated the truth of the Bible. With my near-death experience, it has become my unique understanding to perceive the truth from a different perspective.

Asking again, who do *you* say is Jesus Christ? You are required to have an answer to this question. The answer cannot be rote or a "cadence" where you just spit out the answer, half-mumbled and as fast as you can. God looks at your heart's condition for an answer. To state it bluntly: if Jesus is not in your heart, you are in trouble.

Who is Jesus? If we have to respond to that question to our God, the Father, when we enter eternity, then who is Jesus? A plethora of books have been written about Him. Taking something experienced outside earth and imposing earthly terms, I dare say I will fall short describing how magnificent He is to the world.

Jesus is part of the Triune God. The light I experienced had three combined elements into one being. In the same way, there are three parts to a chicken egg: the shell, the yolk, and the white. Each part of the egg, if used separately, produces unique culinary properties, but all three elements make up one egg. For example, the mineral-rich shell can enrich the soil for enhanced plant growth. The yolk, combined with milk and sugar, makes a delicious, creamy pudding.

The white, whipped to lofty peaks achieves the light, pillowy height of an angel food cake. All three retain different qualities yet perform otherwise, yet they constitute one chicken egg. In the same manner, God the Father, God the Son and God the Spirit are each separate to perform unique tasks, yet they all are one God. I felt each entity as I traveled closer and deeper into the light, with the ability to concentrate on any of the three separately, just as one would recognize each individual person at a family reunion. I knew the Triune God, in its completeness, was the Creator of all things.

For reasoning purposes, I want to pose the argument for the Triune God adopting a classic mathematical formula. Remember in geometry class when the assignment was to determine the size of all the angles using the "if-then" formula: if $A=B$ and $B=C$, then $A=C$? I knew as I moved toward the light, that the light was God, but I could also identify Jesus and the Spirit within the same light. When we speak of God, we also speak of Jesus. And when we speak of the Spirit, we also speak of God. Therefore, the values for the equation are: $A=$ God and $B=$ Spirit and $C=$ Jesus. If God $=$ Spirit and Spirit $=$ Jesus, then God $=$ Jesus.

How do we know this is a true statement? Genesis 1:3 (HCSB): "Now the earth was formless and empty, darkness covered the surface of the watery depths, and the Spirit of God was hovering over the surface of the waters. Then God said, 'let there be light,' and there was light." The Spirit hovered over the formless earth, and then God spoke into the nothingness and created light. Therefore, the Spirit and God had existed before the earth was formed. But where is the third element of the Triune God? John 1:1-3 (ERV): "Before the world began, the Word was there. The Word was with God, and the Word was God. He was there with God in the beginning. Everything was made through him, and nothing was made without him." Because there was nothing before the world began, God used His voice to command the world into existence. His speech, the words He used, ordered all life. First John 1-3 concurs with Genesis 1:3. "The Word became a man and lived among us. We saw His divine greatness—the greatness that belongs to the only Son of the Father. The Word was full of grace and truth" (John 1:14, ERV).

The Word that declared everything into existence became a man and walked on this earth. If the Word was God, then God walked on this earth as a man. The man's name was Jesus. What was "the Word was full of grace and truth"? They are identifiers of Jesus. If Jesus was the "Word" and the "Word" *was* full of grace and truth; then, Jesus was full of grace and truth. Rest assured, we can interpret the words of Jesus as truth. In the book of John, Jesus further identifies himself as God's known name "I AM" as truth. John 8:58 (HCSB): "Jesus said to them, 'I assure you: Before Abraham was, I AM.'"

But who is "I AM"? In the book of Exodus, God identifies himself to Moses at the burning bush. In Exodus 3:14 (NIV), God said to Moses, "I AM who I AM. This is what you are to say to the Israelites: 'I AM has sent me to you.'" But that still does not link us to Abraham in Jesus' identifying statement back in the book of John. Before Abraham, the father of the Israelite nation committed his life to God, he was known as Abram. God came to Abram and identified Himself to Abram. Genesis 17:1 (NIV): "When Abram was ninety-nine years old, the Lord appeared to him and said, 'I AM God Almighty; walk before me faithfully and be blameless.'" Therefore, if "*I AM* God Almighty" identified himself as such to Abraham and as "I AM" to Moses, then when Jesus identifies himself as the "*I AM*" before Abraham, one can argue that Jesus is "*I AM*" because Jesus is full of grace *and truth*.

From this understanding, we can then argue that Jesus was the Son of God. Each one of us has a set of biological parents. If Jesus was a man, then who was His father and mother? The Bible informs us that the Spirit came upon Mary. The same Spirit that hovered over the earth came to Mary, separating the laws of nature to father Jesus. If the Spirit is God, then Jesus is the son of God. Luke 1:35 (NIV): "The angel answered, 'The Holy Spirit will come on you, and the power of the Most High will overshadow you. So the holy one to be born will be called the Son of God.'" The term "son" signifies his family ties. The Jewish religion is patriarchal in family structure. A person's identity was indicated through the father's name: for example, "David-son of Jesse." If people were identified by their name in association with their father's name, then when Jesus says, He is the "Son of God," He is earnestly saying "Jesus-son of God." Jesus is claiming direct lineage by placing God the Father in His name. Just before His death, Jesus discloses who He is to the religious authority of the day, the Sanhedrin.

> The high priest asked Jesus another question: "Are you the Messiah, the Son of the blessed God?" Jesus answered, "Yes, I am the Son of God. And in the future you will see the Son of Man sitting at the right side of God All-Powerful. And you will see the Son of Man coming on the clouds of heaven."
>
> Mark 14:61-62 (ERV)

I need to make it clear here that Jesus is not a half-breed. Nor is Jesus a demi-god, like the fabled Percy Jackson, who had the god Poseidon as his father and Sally Jackson a mere human as his mother. Jesus is fully human and fully God, in a hypostatic union. If Jesus is claiming He is the "I AM" before Abraham, then He is wholly God walking on earth because that is God's precise name. When we share a parent's first *and* last name, we are customarily given a differentiating identifier, such as a nickname or a title of Sr. or Jr. When Jesus says He is the "I AM" in John 8:58, He is claiming His exact name, "God Almighty." Jesus is God, the "I AM" walking on earth in human existence: fully human and fully God. John 10:30 (HCSB): Jesus says, "the Father and I are one." Colossians 1:15 (ESV) proclaims, "He is the image of the invisible God, the firstborn of all creation." John 14:10 (NIV): Jesus says, "Don't you believe that I am in the Father, and that the Father is in me? The words I say to you I do not speak on my own authority. Rather, it is the Father, living in me, who is doing his work."

If Jesus is God, then why did He set himself into His creation by coming to earth? Jesus came to deliver us. He is our hero amid villains. The now-famous scripture that Tim Tebow painted on his eye black for the 2008 National Championship Football game[8], John 3:16 (NKJV) assures us, "For God so loved the world that He gave His only begotten Son, that whoever believes in Him should not perish but have everlasting life." Everlasting life is that life that extends into heaven with God and all the heavenly beings. This earthly life is one that dies and decomposes in the ground, but our hearts and minds travel into heaven to live with our father forever. As mentioned before in a previous chapter, stopping at verse sixteen does not portray the broader picture of God's intention. Verses seventeen and eighteen continue to state the reason Jesus came to earth. John 3:17-18 (ESV) reads (emphasis added):

> For God *did not* send his Son into the world to *condemn* the world, but in order that the world might be *saved through him*. Whoever believes in him *is not condemned*, but whoever does not believe is condemned already, because he has not believed in the name of the only Son of God.

Our God is not a God that hates and punishes at will. He is a God of love, sacrifice, mercy, and justice. He is a God who adores His creation so much that He provided a way for us to continue in our relationship with Him for eternity. He came to earth to celebrate, cry, eat, heal, laugh, rest, teach and touch us.

How many times have you read or heard a story of a parent's sacrifices for a child who was in grave danger? Loving parents perform amazing feats when sparing their children from harm. They will step in front of cars, jump into swimming pools; they would throw their children out of windows of burning houses if needed. Loving parents with a chronically ill child would, at a moment's notice, wholeheartedly exchange places with their child just to prevent their child from suffering. Why? Because the love of a parent is a wonderfully sacrificial love.

The Germans bombed the capital city of London during World War II. To prevent the city's children from harm, the British Government developed a logistical plan to transport the children to protected places in the country. Operation Pied Piper facilitated moving millions of juveniles to homes that had opened up their doors to help raise them during wartime conditions. It was a massive undertaking. Parents, concerned about the family's safety in London, placed their children on trains headed to unknown households to spare them from the ravages of war. A testament to the parental love of many Londoners, this mission was coupled with emotional heartbreak while saving their confused and frightened little ones. As they were loading the young ones on the trains, the parent's questioned if they would ever reunite with their children after the war. More importantly, parents were not guaranteed set living conditions for their young family members at the other end of the train ride. They had to trust the life as a foster child in the countryside was better than a life among the war debris. Moreover, if the mother or father became casualties during a bombing raid, the children would have settled with a foster parent ensuring the continuation of care. Overwhelmingly, the desire to spare their children from the horrors of war prompted many Londoners to relinquish their parental rights.[9] In the end, the enormous sacrificial undertaking by loving parents in Operation Pied Piper was tremendously effective in saving the lives of many war stricken children.

God has much the same love and concern for us. We are His creation. He created this earth for us to enjoy, live, love, and work. His plan was for us to trust Him through our free will, enjoying a relationship formed by love for love. Unfortunately, humankind keeps walking off the path and chooses to experience lives separated from God and His unwavering love for us. We were designed to love

God, but for us to experience His love, we must make an uncoerced choice to trust Him. Since humankind continuously prefers a life that is not God-filled, man forces God Himself to step into His creation to save His children. He had to come to earth and demonstrated to us how to love God and our neighbor. "She [Mary] will give birth to a son. You will name him Jesus. Give him that name because he will save his people from their sins" (Matthew 1:21, ERV). The name Jesus means LORD (Yahweh) saves.[10]

Jesus is our savior. Our God's story is one of love. No other god can claim the love for His children than our God. Since God's light is pure love, only those who accept the love of God in their hearts can enter the kingdom of heaven. Otherwise, heaven would cease as pure love.

So how do we clean our hearts from the darkness, deceit, hate, self-obstruction, and pain of this world? It is only through Christ (God) who died for our lack of understanding of God's kingdom of absolute love so that we can obtain eternal life in heaven. Jesus is the Word, who is the "I AM" before Abraham, and the Word is truth and grace. When Jesus spoke, He declared words of truth from the love in His heart. Jesus was crucified, a horribly agonizing death, for revealing the truth to the people. He was an innocent man put to death because of others' fraudulent statements. Bluntly put: the people in authority in the first century placed God on trial (a fixed one) and killed Him for being truthful. After His death, Jesus showed us life continues beyond this earthly realm by His return to earth to teach His disciples for forty days. There were many eyewitness accounts of His return to earth. The women at His tomb, Cleopas with the other disciple on the Emmaus road, and the disciples in the upper room all bear witness to Jesus's living existence post-mortem.

I remember in seventh grade when we were given an assignment to take a sample of cells from inside our cheeks. Using a toothpick, we were to scape the soft tissue from inside our mouths and place the sample on a slide. We were to place the slide on the microscope and sketch what we observed. Many students scraped the inside of their cheeks so hard they drew blood. Our science teacher, attempting to prevent students from further injury, inquired as to why they were digging so aggressively. When several students replied it was because they could not see anything on the toothpick, my teacher loudly responded, "That's why you have the microscope! Can your eyes see microscopically? *No!*" God chose to walk on this earth to prove to us there is much more to life than what man has feebly projected.

There are several worlds unseen to our human eyes; microscopic and macroscopic. Jesus came to show us the unseen world of heaven. The key to getting to heaven is the belief that Jesus was God who came to demonstrate to us there was more to God's creation than just what we could visualize. Jesus is the doorway to eternal life in heaven. Second Timothy 1:10 (ERV): "And now it has been shown to us in the coming of our Savior Christ Jesus. He destroyed death and showed us the way to have life. Yes, through the Good News, Jesus showed us the way to have life that cannot be destroyed." John the Baptist announces to us who Jesus was and His mission in this world. John 1:29 (HCSB): "...John saw Jesus coming toward him and said, 'Here is the Lamb of God, who takes away the sin of the world!'" Through the belief in Jesus, his teachings, and what He accomplished for all people, you can gain eternal life with Him in Heaven.

God gifted us Jesus as a man who lived among us and taught all who would listen. There is much more to God's creation than what we know. Through His death, He becomes our sacrifice to God, humanity's "payment" to God. "These children are people with physical bodies. So Jesus himself became like them and had the same experiences they have. Jesus did this so that, by dying, he could destroy the one who has the power of death—the devil" (Hebrews 2:14, ERV).

Initially, Cain and Abel were to present gifts to God to thank Him for all that God provided for each of them. Abel had the livestock, and Cain had the grain harvest. As time progressed, animals or grain were given to thank God or to ask God for absolution for failing to live, according to God's plan (what we call sin), all coordinated by the Jewish high priests. Here is the incredibly awesome aspect of just how wonderful is our God. God decided that He was going to do away with all the sacrifices and came down as Jesus (our High Priest) to sacrifice himself in the place of our sacrifices. "He doesn't need to offer sacrifices every day, as high priests do—first for their own sins, then for those of the people. He did this once for all when He offered Himself" (Hebrews 7:27, HCSB). Once Jesus's blood touched the ground, it cleansed the earth from the blood of the slain Abel; it also cleansed the earth from all the wrongful deaths of others. First John 1:7 (ERV) instructs, "We should live in the light, where God is. If we live in the light, we have fellowship with each other, and the blood sacrifice of Jesus, God's Son, washes away every sin and makes us clean." "For the wages of sin is death, but the gift of God is eternal life in Christ Jesus our Lord" (Romans 6:23, NIV).

Back to the first test question: Who do you declare is Jesus Christ? Jesus proposed this question to Peter, one of His disciples. Peter had been with Jesus, as Jesus taught, healed, feed, casted out demons, laughed, and cried with Him. Peter walked and talked with God on earth, and yet Jesus had to ask him this identical question. Mark 8:29 (ERV): "'But what about you?' he asked. 'Who do you say I am?' Peter answered, 'You are the Messiah.'" Who do you say is Jesus? You have to figure out the answer here on earth because by the time you cross over, it is too late.

Question number two on the final exam is: with the life you were given, what did you do with it? This is a question my mother often repeated during my childhood years. It is a precisely equalizing question. If you were poor and undereducated, what did you do with it? If you were rich and well-schooled, what did you do with it? If you were physically disabled in some way, what did you do with it? If you were raised with injustices all around you, what did you do with it? If you were given health, what did you do with it? If you knew the ways of the world, what did you do with it? If you were given talents and gifts, what did you do with them? If you believed in Jesus, what did you do with it?

It is in this question that we are held accountable for all of our actions and inactions, emotions, and feelings. All of the accountability in our lives, from beginning to end, lies in the answer to this question. Some of us should say "ouch" right about now because we know we have fallen short and could have done better. Good news! You can change this minute and enjoy a better life with Jesus. When you go to God the Father, you can faithfully and honestly answer that you know Him. First John 3:7 (ERV): "Dear children, don't let anyone lead you into the wrong way. Christ always did what was right. So to be good like Christ, you must do what is right." Romans 5:9 (ERV): "We have been made right with God by the blood sacrifice of Christ. So through Christ, we will surely be saved from God's anger."

After I was told to "go back because there was more for me to do," I realized we are here to do work. We are to deliberately and selectively choose actions, thoughts, and feelings that reflect the glory of God. If we are accountable for our life's actions, then what type of life can we live and be right with God? First, *everyone* who is beyond the age of accountability has sinned, Christian or not. Believe me, my list of shameful deeds can fill volumes, but each day I try to get it right and represent a better reflection of Jesus. "...[A]ll have sinned and fall short of the glory of God" (Romans 3:23, NIV).

I began this story by describing the time my brother restrained me underwater. My brother grew out of his adolescent years and matured into a compassionate and responsible adult, a gentle giant of sorts. He is a devoted father to two beautiful children and a God-fearing husband who shares his faith with his community. I forgave my brother a long time ago for imprisoning me under the water and for all the other ignorant stuff towards me. Why? Because God has forgiven me for all the senseless stuff I have done to him and others. I bet most of us can recount some extremely distressing stories of how we have fallen short of the Glory of God. News flash: we all have our paddles in the water, rowing the same boat named sin.

How do we enjoy a life that is worthy of God and our neighbor? Colossians 3:2-4 (ERV): "Think only about what is up there, not what is here on earth. Your old self has died, and your new life is kept with Christ in God. Yes, Christ is now your life, and when he comes again, you will share in His glory." We are to stop living in the world and achieving what the world conceives is right. The world and all its ways will always steer you in the wrong direction.

> So put everything evil out of your life: sexual sin, doing anything immoral, letting sinful thoughts control you, and wanting things that are wrong. And don't keep wanting more and more for yourself, which is the same as worshiping a false god. God will show his anger against those who don't obey him, because they do these evil things.
>
> Colossians 3:5-6 (ERV)

When we receive Christ in our hearts, we want to reflect Him by not having anger or slander towards others. No more lies and deceit for our own gain, but rather we desire a life, which is the image of Christ. John 14:20 (NIV): "On that day you will realize that I am in my Father, and you are in me, and I am in you." Through our commitment to Christ, we all collectively become one body of believers who cast away the world's darkness and walk in the ways of Christ.

> God has chosen you and made you his holy people. He loves you. So your new life should be like this: Show mercy to others. Be kind, humble, gentle, and patient. Don't be angry with each other, but forgive each other. If you feel someone has wronged you, forgive them. Forgive others because the Lord forgave you. Together with these things, the most important part of your new life is to love each other. Love is what holds everything together

in perfect unity. Let the peace that Christ gives control your thinking. It is for peace that you were chosen to be together in one body. And always be thankful. Let the teaching of Christ live inside you richly. Use all wisdom to teach and counsel each other. Sing psalms, hymns, and spiritual songs with thankfulness in your hearts to God. Everything you say and everything you do should be done for Jesus your Lord. And in all you do, give thanks to God the Father through Jesus.

Colossians 3:12-17 (ERV)

Lottie Moon, a Christian missionary, was instrumental in developing the missionary field of service for the Southern Baptist conference while serving in China during the late 1800s-early 1900s. Lottie was thirty-three years old when she accepted her role as a missionary. She died at the age of seventy-two aboard a ship in the Japanese Harbor of Kōbe, having served as a missionary for thirty-nine years. Lottie poured her life into the Chinese country, constantly preaching the Word of God to the communities. She focused her work on women and children, but on hearing the message of Jesus; the men would gather on the other side of makeshift walls and intently listen to the Good News.[11] Lottie would write in her Missional Journal:

> I feel that I would gladly give my life to working among such a people and regard it as a joy and privilege. Yet, to women who may think of coming, I would say, count well the cost. You must give up all that you hold dear and live a life that is, outside of your work, narrow and contracted to the last degree. If you really love the work, it will atone for all you give up, and when your work is ended, and you go Home, to see the Master's smile and hear his voice of welcome will more than repay your toils amid the heathen. [12]

A life following Jesus is not an easy one. Then again, Jesus never promised us a life of ease, just a life that would be worth it. Lottie

Moon's journal entry is a superb example of how we as Christians have to surrender a life of customs and security to perform the great commission the Lord Jesus set out for us. If God is creator, then all belongs to Him. If all belongs to Him, then are we really giving up anything? Remember, we cannot take any of our belongings to heaven, just our hearts and minds. Plenty of Egyptian tombs contain overwhelming proof that when you die, you leave your stuff behind. The harvest is great, but the workers are few. With the life you were granted, what did you do with it?

I do not want you caught in the dark void as I was when I transferred over. It is an awful and isolated existence. I do not want you to have to cry out for God amid a blackness so dark you are lost within it. When you believe, you are able to go to the light and experience the blessed, pure love of God Almighty.

One final note: when you believe in Jesus as our Lord and Savior, your belief will be greater than mine could ever be. You see, I have seen the light. I know it exists. I can identify how it feels. I know the light is the Triune God. All of you who have merely heard and read the Word and believe, express a markedly greater level of faith than I do. My faith can only ride on your faith jacket's coattails. Honorable and unwavering faith is far more powerful if it comes without seeing. I have seen and believed. You have heard and believed. Jesus tells His disciple Thomas after he had touched Jesus' hands and side, "...'you believe because you see me. Great blessings belong to the people who believe without seeing me!'" (John 20:29, NIV).

Here is the Final Exam:
1) Who do you say is Jesus?
2) With the life you were given, what did you do with it?

The Salvation

"...God chose us to have salvation through our Lord Jesus Christ."
1 Thessalonians 5:9

Salvation, as per the American Heritage Dictionary, is "preservation or deliverance from evil or difficulty or...the deliverance from the power or penalty of sin."[13] Zechariah, prophesying over his newborn son, John, said, "You will make his people understand that they will be saved by having their sins forgiven" (Luke 1:77, ERV). "His people" is addressing the Lord's people. All those who believe in Jesus as the Messiah who came to redeem the world from sin.

What is sin, and why do we need saving from it? "Anyone who sins breaks God's law. Yes, sinning is the same as living against God's law" (1 John 3:4, ERV). Since they executed Jesus (God, the Word and Truth) for crimes He did not commit, the people put to death an innocent man. During His ministry, Jesus stood up to the religious authority when that authority, over time, distorted and manipulated God's laws for their own purposes and control. Jesus came to place humankind back on God's authentic, faithful path by clearing out the religious partisan views that had evolved since the law was given through Moses. God provided the law to His people, the Israelites (Jewish), to separate them from all other people to accomplish His work in the world. God's people were to represent God to the rest of the world so that the rest of the world would follow suit and replicate the example. Needless to say, that did not happen because God's people kept interjecting their former way of life back into their lives. However, because our God is an all-knowing God, He knew that man would continue to break the law after Adam and Eve sinned in the garden. God, through Jesus, came to earth to physically communicate with us and demonstrate to us how to live as God's people. What did the people do when He was on earth? They killed Him.

Yet in His death, He revealed to us the most extravagant gift, the gift of an eternal life with Him in heaven. After Jesus had died, He returned to earth to teach all those who believed, reassuring them there is more than what we achieve, experience, and perceive here on earth. Jesus came to explain to us that our God is a supreme God who created us with a purpose and is with us in our ordinary lives. God never abandons us; He never forsakes us. Moreover, He is a God that loves and cares for His children in all things. Our God created us to have a reciprocal relationship with Him. He loves us, and we, in turn, have to believe to receive this gift of love and compassion. Exclusively through the life and death of Jesus, can we harbor hope against our punishment for breaking His laws. No other god can claim this lifesaving characteristic.

> The people who believe that Jesus is the Messiah are God's children. Anyone who loves the Father also loves the Father's children. How do we know that we love God's children? We know because we love God and we obey his commands [laws]. Loving God means obeying his commands. And God's commands are not too hard for us, because everyone who is a child of God has the power to win against the world.

> 1 John 5:1-4 (ERV)

We know God is a benevolent God. We recognize this because God looked down on the world and said it was good. "So God made every kind of animal. He made the wild animals, the tame animals, and all the small crawling things. And God saw that this was good" (Genesis 1:25, ERV). What God created was good. "God's thundering voice is amazing! He does great things that we cannot understand" (Job 37:5, ERV). Jesus identifies God as good in the gospel of Matthew "A man came to Jesus and asked, 'Teacher, what good thing must I do to have eternal life?' Jesus answered, 'Why do you ask me about what is good? Only God is good. But if you want to have eternal life, obey the law's commands'" (Matthew 19:16-17, ERV). Remember, previous arguments proved that Jesus is the Word and the Word is truth. When Jesus says, "only God is good," then it is true. Our God is good.

So, what is the problem? Just obey the laws of God, and then we can live with God in heaven. What is problematic to humankind is it has a sin problem. People seem to never completely follow the laws. Many times, the ways of the world seem more appealing than the ways of God. Even a two-year-old will lie about how many times the hand has been in the cookie jar. Life just seems better when you have three cookies instead of the two you have been given. This is an elementary example, but it clarifies how easy all of us fall away from the law; it is in our nature. When Jesus walked on this earth, He simplified the ten laws into two: love God and love your neighbor. Nonetheless, we still get it wrong.

If we always do wrong, as per God's laws, then how do we make our lives right with God and gain eternal life with Him in heaven? As when you receive a ticket for breaking traffic laws by speeding on the highway, and you incur the penalty. There is a penalty for sin, and that penalty is death or, worse yet, hell, an eternal state of misery and pain in the absence of God.

When I taught school and assisting my own children with their own academics, I would compose a word from the test answers: an acronym. Many pastors and Bible teachers have employed the similar technique to help others with their faith walk in their churches and Bible classes. I think "Do CPR-S" is especially appropriate since I am discussing the heart's condition throughout this writing.

Do-pray to God
C-Confess you are a sinner
P-Profess Jesus as your Lord and Savior
R-Repent of your ways.
S-Spread the Good News

1) *Do* pray to God. First Thessalonians 5:17 instructs us to never stop praying. Humankind has prayed to God since the time of Enosh, the grandchild of Adam and Eve (Genesis 4:26, HCSB). More importantly, our prayers do not stay here on earth. The book of Revelation illustrates for us that the prayers of God's people advance to heaven. "The smoke from the incense went up from the angel's hand to God. The smoke went up with the prayers of God's people" (Revelation 8:4, ERV). Your prayer does not just float out into nothingness, it goes to God. It is the best form of instant messaging ever created, and God invented it thousands of years before man figured it out electronically. When you pray for the first time, ask Jesus to come into your heart. That is your starting point.

2) C-confess you are a sinner. "But no, all have strayed away; all are rotten with sin. Not one is good, not one!" (Psalm 14:3 TLB). "Yes, all have sinned; all fall short of God's glorious ideal;" (Romans 3:23 TLB). I routinely say, "Lord, I can never get it right in this life. Help me to understand how to do this, teach me." Say whatever *you* need to in your confession to God. Admit you have not placed God first in your heart and that you have not appreciated your neighbor. Remember, this is your prayer to God, and you must employ *your* words that generate from *your* heart. The condition of the heart is the vital statistic of Christianity.

3) P-profess Jesus as your Lord and Savior. There is no collective salvation, meaning your Christian friend cannot secure you into heaven. You do not get into heaven because you were part of a group that went and picked up trash on the beach last Thursday. No good deed list gets checked off for an entrance fee into heaven. Works do

not produce an admissions ticket. You cannot buy your way into heaven. You get yourself into heaven based on your faith in Jesus Christ and professing to others that you believe in Him. You must believe Jesus was the Son of God.

> For if you tell others with your own mouth that Jesus Christ is your Lord and believe in your own heart that God has raised him from the dead, you will be saved. For it is by believing in his heart that a man becomes right with God; and with his mouth he tells others of his faith, confirming his salvation.

> Romans 10:9-10 (TLB)

At present, many people believe Jesus was a prominent philosopher, maybe even a prophet. This belief is not going to obtain eternal life. It is the belief that Jesus—fully human and fully God— walked on this earth, suffered on the cross, died an innocent man, and became alive again to show us life exists beyond this earthly plane. It is because of *this* belief you allow Jesus to direct the rest of your life.

4) R-repent of your sins. Sadly, this is where vast numbers of Christians fall short in their faith walk. Christians, in the multitude, understand prayer is critical for a relationship with God. They fervently confess that they have done wrong. They speak of Jesus in their hearts, but their behavior never changes. They *never* become the new person Christ invites us to become when we choose Him over the world. Regretfully, some churches embrace people who never stop committing adultery, cheating, lying, stealing, coveting their neighbor's house, cars, or checking accounts. They are not very good representatives of Christ. Why? Because people never transformed their ways. Once we have honestly asked Christ in our hearts, we want to reflect Him in all ways. That means we reshape the way we behave, communicate, listen, analyze situations, manage our bodies for nourishment, and solve problems. We are new persons in Christ. He is in us, and we are in Him. If we believe this is genuine, then we

need to look and act as if we have Christ in us. Be wise in choosing a church that helps you reflect your new person in Christ. You will require the church's help to remain on God's path. As the body of Christ, we must link arms in support to nurture us on the righteous path of God and keep our faithful accountable.

My heart aches for this generation inculcated by social media. As I was growing up and making senseless mistakes, I did not have to relive them, as do so many in this young generation. If I messed up or uttered something wrong, and no one heard it or recalled it socially, I was absolved of my mistake. Indeed, I still had to seek forgiveness from God, but I could get up the next day and go to school without much head drama. In today's world, if a child or young adult's mistake is captured on video, the blunder is on a never-ending loop throughout the social media sites. It is cruelty at its greatest. Woefully, the gaffe or infraction is available for the world to watch for years to come. While social media's intent is for good, I dare say it is disappointingly manipulated to destroy our precious youth. How do our children pick themselves up when their life's most embarrassing moments are now the world's belly laughs? How lonely must these children feel when their hubris communities at large perceive them as a joke or judge them harshly? We all make mistakes, but through God's mercy, we are pardoned from our wrongdoings. Jesus offers us hope. We learn from our faults and forgive ourselves as God forgave us when humanity placed Jesus on the cross. God could have condemned all of mankind for executing the innocent Jesus, but He did not because God knew we did not thoroughly comprehend our actions. As a newly created person in Christ, we must learn to produce a healthy Christian environment for ourselves and our families.

It is critical for the church to support each other as we walk through our lives. We encounter challenges at every turn. Narrowly, through faith in Jesus do we become one with Him. Christ presents a second chance in life. When someone believes in Jesus and His saving grace, then the person is born again. Everyone is born through a natural birth, but when we elect Jesus, the Holy Spirit births us again.

> There was a man named Nicodemus, one of the Pharisees. He was an important Jewish leader. One night he came to Jesus and said, "Teacher, we know that you are a teacher sent from God. No one can do these miraculous signs that you do unless they have God's help." Jesus answered, "I assure you, everyone must be born again. Anyone who is not born again cannot be in God's kingdom."...The only life people get from their human parents is physical. But the new life that the Spirit gives a person is spiritual.

> John 3:1-3, 6 (ESV)

Find a pastor in a church that will baptize you. The baptism does not save your eternal soul; that is achieved by faith in Jesus. Baptism is an outward expression of what you carry in your heart. Jesus' cousin John baptized Him. Jesus' disciples baptized believers as the Christian church grew. Just like Jesus, we employ the practice of baptizing believers today. Recognize when you undertake this, Jesus prayed for *you* to become one with Him. My favorite prayer is the one when Jesus prayed for all of us just before His death in John 17. Decipher the words carefully and follow the pattern that Jesus generates. Read how dynamic and wonderful this prayer conveys Jesus' love for all who believe.

> I am not praying for these alone but also for the future believers who will come to me because of the testimony of these. My prayer for all of them is that they will be of one heart and mind, just as you and I are, Father—that just as you are in me and I am in you, so they will be in us, and the world will believe you sent me.
> I have given them the glory you gave me—the glorious unity of being one, as we are— I in them and you in me, all being perfected into one—so that the world will know you sent me and will understand that you love them as much as you love me. Father, I want them with me—these you've given me—so that they can see

my glory. You gave me the glory because you loved me before the world began!

John 17:20-24 (TLB)

5) Spread the Good News! Time is of an essence and we require all believers' accomplishing the work of the LORD. We do not know when Jesus will return to this earth, coming from the clouds in glory. "Then the sign of the Son of Man will appear in the sky, and then all the peoples of the earth will mourn; and they will see the Son of Man coming on the clouds of heaven with power and great glory" (Matthew 24:30, HCSB). We are not supposed to know. There is a compelling reason for this. If we knew when Jesus was going to return, we would stop doing the work of the Lord. If high schoolers can barely work at the end of the school year, Christians would flatly walk off the job. Why work when, in a couple of years, Jesus will return? People would see the work as fruitless. We are to do the work of the Lord, spreading the Good News to all ends of the earth until the day of Jesus' arrival. Until that time,

> But to do this, you will need the strong belt of truth and the breastplate of God's approval. Wear shoes that are able to speed you on as you preach the Good News of peace with God. In every battle you will need faith as your shield to stop the fiery arrows aimed at you by Satan. And you will need the helmet of salvation and the sword of the Spirit—which is the Word of God. Pray all the time. Ask God for anything in line with the Holy Spirit's wishes. Plead with him, reminding him of your needs, and keep praying earnestly for all Christians everywhere.
>
> Ephesians 6:14-18 (TLB)

The Lesser gods

"Instead of honoring the divine greatness of God, who lives forever, they traded it for the worship of idols—things made to look like humans, who get sick and die, or like birds, animals, and snakes."
Romans 1:23 (ERV)

Humankind has constantly struggled with recognizing God as their almighty God. Our unbound will to choose to love God gets in the way of our choosing. Repeatedly, when we become disenchanted or questioning, we seek lesser gods for an expeditious response. In our electronic age, we require immediate feedback. If our friends, colleagues, family members can text us back within a minute or two, then our gods should respond in the same manner, right? The problem is that including these gods, or a lack of a god, never completely answers our questions and never delivers a resolution to our problems. The true God works on your heart's condition, not the condition of your wallet, school project, or whatever your ailment is at the time of your distress. Our hearts are like large cruise ships that take time to turn around. While our personal ships are changing course, we are busy eating, drinking, gambling, shopping, and entertaining ourselves in all the ways of the world.

When I taught school, the administration instructed all the teaching staff to honor every student's belief story as truth. As might be expected, having experienced a near-death experience, it was impossible for me to remain silent when students would profess an alternate belief system. As a teacher, I felt it was my job to expose the truth to my students. Whenever a student inquired of me about death, I would tell them about my experience in the light of God. No student objected to my story and called it false, nor did I have one parent report me to the school board. Typically, in fact, I had more students come to me between classes to hastily ask me more about God and my experience. The students were eager for truth. The idea that our youth need to explore all the different faiths to figure out which one is "their" truth is a bunch of hogwash. It simply encourages children to scream louder for the truth in the midst of their confusion. Here is my question to all those who feel "all belief systems" represent "a" truth; do you like being lied to? Because this concept of living in a circular door of faith does nothing but lie to our youth and exacerbates their confusion and loneliness.

When one of my students would proclaim a non-Christian god or atheism as truth, I would habitually ask them why they believed the way they did. This is a terrific starting point since I would get a feel for their belief's foundation. Sometimes belief was determined because a family member had a persuasive influence over the person, or the student had read a dynamic, thought-provoking book. I had to propose a couple of "why" questions before I recounted my story. Just like God does not force us to worship Him, we, as witnesses to Christ, cannot force people to believe. The proper "why" question is a question addressing the heart. Once people have confidence that you are not going to stomp on their hearts, they are more willing to share their beliefs with you. Otherwise, they are in fight-or-flight mode in defense of your deluge of theology. Ideally, you want them to ask *you* a why question in return so that you can slide Jesus into the conversation. I caution you not to browbeat people with the Bible. The Bible is a tool we implement in our religion; it is not our religion. Our religion is worshiping the Triune God: God the Father, God the Son, and God the Holy Spirit. This is why we can write in our Bibles, a practice that is highly encouraged by the faithful.

Up to this point, the story has been about our love for God and its genuineness. The following section pertains to our love for our family, friends, and neighbors. Through a cursory comparison of other faiths, we gather a deeper understanding of the power and strength of our mighty God. To prevent this book from becoming a five-hundred-page paperweight, I have included a brief "self-help" apologetic index of popular, non-Christian religions to help start the conversations. Each faith heading on its own is worthy of an entire discourse explaining how it does not fully compare with the sacrifice, mercy, and justice of the one Triune Christian God. With the world conditioned to messages having a limited character count, a detailed comparison needs a reservation for another book. If the reader so desires to find out more information on a particular religion's assessment, there are plenty of other resources on comparative theology.

As previously mentioned, I believe we are getting limited on time before our Lord appears for His church. Utilize this section for guidance when talking with friends of various faiths. I would prefer my friends and family in heaven with me, and I am sure you do as well. The exclusive way to enter heaven and eternal life is to know the truth of the Gospels and fall in love with Jesus. Here is a simple guide to begin the "why" questions.

Atheism—usually known as a denial of God but more of a skepticism of God. Try to find out the difference in the person and begin to question from there. If they are a skeptic, they need to be shown who is God. Ask them about things that correlate in their lives. Why do you think when you question something, the answer appears within a day or so in maybe a road sign or in someone's side conversation? That is not an accident. Ask our friends about the beauty of the earth and skies. Why is the sky so beautiful on a clear night? Make mention of the extraordinary feat that it took to put everything in balance and order. How, in a room of crying babies, a mother can identify her own child's cry? How is that possible? Our God hears and identifies our cry as being His children.

For the skeptic, God is there; the person merely requires God pointed out to them. It may take some persistence in pointing God out on your part, but the heart will begin to analyze from our God's perspective. Why? Because love is in our design. A child without question will say, I love you and give you a hug because it is our human nature to love. A loving God made humanity. For the skeptic atheist, the task is to get them thinking about who God is and how God works.

For the adamant non-believer of God, usually there is tremendous pain associated in their lives or a fright of being held accountable. They throw themselves into science and technology, making modern electronics and scientific equations their substitute God. Belief in God is a fool's game since there is no practical way to prove God's existence. They crave more and more technology until death, when "lights are turned out," or someone is "powered off."

Figuring out the difference in atheists might require a number of why questions. Take caution to 1—not give up on these individuals, and 2—be prepared for the aggressive responses to the why questions as they arise. If pain or painful injustice is the basis of non-belief, then question about why should we care if there is no God? What makes humankind care about those that suffer? If there is no God who understands caring, then how did humans develop the emotion to care about our loved ones or children, especially those who suffer with terminal illnesses? We care because God molded us in His image, and He is a God that cares.

The pressing question is with the life you were granted, what did you do with it? With the witnessed suffering, what conditions changed? The world's inner cities are plagued with downtrodden conditions. The atheist says there is no God because of all the pain and suffering in the world, but yet many do nothing to combat the pain and suffering. Some atheists take part in social betterment projects, but then the question becomes, why? Why is there a need to better life for someone if there is nothing else to this world? Why have morals when there is no moral accountability? Because it is desirable to help others? Who determines right from wrong? The government? But yet world governments routinely steal from the tax base, misuse funds, and overwhelmingly suppress populations.

For an atheist who is troubled by accountability with their life, be ever so gentle in encouraging them so they can pass the test. This book has provided the only two questions on the final exam. Our God knew we would be tempted with ill-gotten choices, and yet He came to earth to be for us. Jesus made known to us that when we choose Him amid the useless choices around us, we would be given the gift of eternal life with Him in heaven. Inquire as to why the person feels all is lost and nothing restored. If restoration to cars, furniture, and a house is possible, then why cannot the heart? Instinctively, they know a person is far more valuable than a car. Confronting what we have done or what we have said that was improper does not have to intimated us. Admission to wrong is not the atheist's problem; it is the pain associated with the admission that is the scary issue. The steps to accountability do not have to focus on pain, just honesty. From there, the truth will flow. As Christian, we need to give our atheist friends much encouragement and time to answer the why questions. A magnificent beginning for our atheist friend's faith walk is the truth in Proverbs and the poetry of Ecclesiastes. These two books address much of their heart issues.

Buddhism—these are beautifully peaceful people who live their lives focused on the eventual death of which we all must participate. Positivity is the center of all life, with gentle kindness for life's Karma to exert a favorable effect on one's afterlife. Each of us is on our own life path that causes us to choose our end-life Karma. If people would eliminate all wants and desires, then the desired state of life (a life without suffering and pain) is achieved, and Karma is maximized. Life becomes about removing our humanism for a satisfactory result. However, this is problematic since we are human with human qualities. Why must we deny our humanism? Our heart is beautifully made for a relationship with our God, despite our brokenness.

I remember being invited to a Buddhist class and a following worship service, an experience that has exerted a resonating effect on me still today. The chants were mesmerizing as they increased in duration during the worship service. I found my head start to spin as each strike of the gong sounded. The chant of the people created such a soundwave that moved throughout the room that my body felt as if I was on a ship during an angry storm. The people-filled room was heavy in concentration as each person tried to focus on suppressing their minds in their feeble attempt to completely remove themselves from the world. Whereas I am convinced many well-practiced Buddhists can center their minds, I find it interesting a sounding gong is implemented for re-centering the follower's mental thoughts. Evidently, the Buddhists know it is a challenging task to remove all thoughts from one's mind, otherwise, there would be no need for the gong. The service was about the removal of self from the world by having the right mindset, attitude, behavior, thoughts, to find Nirvana. Where is Nirvana? What does it look like? When do we achieve Nirvana?

Our God tells us what heaven is like. He gifted us the Bible to help us understand what heaven looks like and who resides there. The Bible is our written compass, directing us to God. God created us with a thinking mind. He does not want us to extract all thought; rather, concentrate our thoughts on Him. God wants us to know about Him. He desires us to come to Him amid our humanism to be one with Him in His Heaven. In Christianity, far more questions about the afterlife and its "karma" are answered with the Bible than in the mantras of Buddhism. Have patience with our Buddhist friends as they begin understanding eternal life through Jesus Christ. Christianity is about love and peace to all within the human condition, not removed from it. Because of the wisdom found within its quotes, the book of Proverbs is an excellent starting point for a conversation among our good-hearted Buddhist friends.

Confucius/Taoist—more of a political thought and philosophy than a religion. Confucianism and Taoism are about control, because humankind is basically wrong in thought and deed. When humans have complete unselfishness, perfection is achieved. Everyone must suppress their own thoughts, desires, and needs for the greater good of society and better relationships. To obtain the ideal society, humans must concentrate on repeated actions and activities to perfect and remove all human aspects. Supreme harmony (utopia), void of any human imperfection, represents the ideal situation.[14] While this is a superb ideological quest to try to acquire, it still begs the question as to why humans have to remove their humanism for personal betterment and achieve a superior status?

Jesus entered a shattered world, resolving its brokenness by His death and resurrection *as a human*. He suffered on the cross just like we suffer in our losses and pain, to show us the more noble life is with God, the father. This world is not all there is to life, and the world will never be perfect until Christ returns and a new heaven and a new earth's formation. Confucianism and Taoism place believers on an unattainable quest because of humanity's nature. The philosophies urge an answering of the question: when will humanity attain the goal of unselfishness to establish harmony for all? Is it even attainable? Why work so hard to attain perfect non-humanism when our particular makeup is a human existence?

The ultimate harmony in Utopia cannot be achieved because it is our nature to sin and fall away from the laws of God. How many years has man attempted to remove all the wrong thoughts and deeds from one's life? Has man moved any closer to perfect harmony? With the two world wars and countless other wars, the criminal and murderous activities of Stalin, Mao Tse Tung, Idi Amin, Pol Pot, and Castro's communist government, I dare say the compilation of humanity is slipping further and further away from any type of harmony. Jesus had warned us about humanity's disintegration on this earth before He left. It is only through Christ that we can find a solution to our selfishness. He understands how broken we are. Be gentle when asking these friends if they are getting closer to their unselfishness.

Is humanity around them getting any closer to perfection? Just how much work will it take to completely be in harmony? Like our Buddhist friends, learning from the book of Proverbs can open the door for new-found opportunities with Christ.

Feminism—peculiar as this topic may seem, God is rejected based on the oppression of women by men in the religious orders and traditional churches. Many traditional faiths practice complementarianism which is "the theological view that although men and women are created equal in their being and personhood, they are created to complement each other via different roles and responsibilities as manifested in marriage, family life, religious leadership, and elsewhere."[15] These religious affiliates ban women from leadership positions such as priests, pastors, elders, bishops, and the like. Women take a religious stance against the church and God due to lack of leadership roles for them. As a form of retaliation, women choose an absolute rejection of God based on man's behavior.

Many societies are usually male-dominated and patriarchal in design as well. Historically, the oppression of women stems from economic, educational, political, and social suppression. Even today, we discover signs around the world where women are explicitly rejected from achieving their maximum potential using their Godly-given gifts and talents. These women harbor feelings of loathing for all men, for the purposeful maneuvering of women out of potential success within society. This emotional knee-jerk reaction is understandable. Even when God walked on this earth, He came as the son of God, not the daughter of God. I do not think God's intent was to belittle women or coerce them into a second class.

When God formed Eve from the rib of Adam, He did so to create only one humanity. If God had created Eve separately from Adam utilizing a different pile of dirt, there would be two separate human lines. The separate creation of the two would have fabricated chaos from the start. Which lineage would enjoy more power and be more favored by God? God chose to mold Eve from Adam's rib, so there is only *one* humanity and that *all* of humankind is reflective of His image for His purpose. I can honestly claim I am created in the image of God, just like my brothers can. In addition, the Adam who went to sleep and the Adam who woke up after Eve's creation represent two unique Adams. The first created Adam, who came from the dirt, had a larger rib cage than the Adam that awoke. The one that woke up was Adam in a lesser form and therefore was a different Adam. The Adam that awoke was a subordinate of the original Adam, just as Eve was. *Both* of them were created from the original Adam. Moreover, when Adam and Eve sinned in the garden, they each had to snatch a bite of the fruit. Humanity, *in its fullness*, sinned in the garden.

> The woman could see that the tree was beautiful and the fruit looked so good to eat. She also liked the idea that it would make her wise. So she took some of the fruit from the tree and ate it. Her husband was there with her, so she gave him some of the fruit, and he ate it. Then it was as if their eyes opened, and they saw things differently. They saw that they were naked. So they got some fig leaves, sewed them together, and wore them for clothes.
>
> Genesis 3:6-7 (ERV)

A brief mention of Lilith is needed at this point. The folklore of Lilith has become increasingly popular among our pro-feminine groups. With the all-women musical festival known as the Lilith Fair gaining in annual attendance, the need for addressing the subject of Lilith is a critical one. The legend states that before Eve's creation, God formed Lilith (Adam's first wife) from the same dirt as was Adam. She was his full counterpart in all ways except for sexual identity. After her first look at Adam, a struggle of who was greater ensued. Lilith refused Adam as a partner in the Garden of Eden. Because of her refusal, God discharged her from the garden, and she, in turn, took up residence in the Red Sea.[16] With Lilith disposed of, God created a second wife for Adam, this time choosing to form Eve from Adam's rib. This is absolute nonsense and needs to remain in the folklore genre. Eve was Adam's first and only wife.

From the beginning, in the garden, Eve's testimony possessed weight to it. God questioned Eve directly; He did not examine Adam to obtain Eve's statement. Genesis 3:13 (ERV) reads, "Then the LORD God said to the woman, 'What have you done?' She said, 'The snake tricked me, so I ate the fruit.'" God spoke directly to Eve. He judged her and sentenced a punishment only to her and the feminine side of humanity by giving women pain during childbirth. Adam's behavior was also judged and sentenced to labor for not correcting Eve's behavior. *All* of humanity had been delivered a sentence for defiant behavior. God did not play favorites between Adam and Eve, nor was one testimony greater or had more value than the other. Pointedly, God judged the serpent and sentenced it *without* a testimony. Both Adam and Eve could defend themselves individually to God, whereas the serpent was forbidden to voice a defense. God accepted the words of humanity as value and proclaimed a sentence on the serpent based on Adam and Eve's words.

When God decides to walk on this earth, fully human and fully God, He has to obtain Mary's (Jesus' mother) permission to perform the miracle. As the Creator of all things, God had the ability to permit anything He so desired, but He did not. Women were so valuable to God that God asked for the permission from a woman to enter the world to redeem it. When Jesus walked on this earth and talked to women, their testimony *always* carried as much weight as a man's. It was the women that stayed at the foot of the cross to witness the death of Christ. When Jesus was not in the tomb after His death, it was the women who told of Christ's resurrection to the other male disciples. Yes, a woman may have initiated the fall out of the garden, but women fulfilled a deciding role in the saving of the world.

Many interpret the letter to the church in Corinth by Paul as degrading to women. Let's address the confusing passage of 1 Corinthians 11:1-16. In this scripture, Paul is talking about the newly established first-century church's customs in the middle of the major port city of Corinth, in south-central Greece. Corinth was bustling with people from all walks of life during the 1st Century due to its geographical design as an isthmus. In his letter, Paul was trying to teach the new Christian church how to behave as Christians.

In my opinion, many analysts fail when interpreting this passage because they do not take into account the bio-economics of first-century Corinth. Bio-economic meaning the conditions of health for a person and the community. These conditions include congenital birth defects, disease, medicine, nutrition, access to clean water for cooking and bathing, cleanliness of living conditions, as well as all the money and logistical infrastructure to sustain a healthy lifestyle.

The Christian church was open to Jews and Gentile alike. It was the meshing of the two lifestyles that Paul needed to discuss with the church. Some members were affluent, while others were dirt poor. Paul needed to gather everyone on the same page and maintain consistent behavior to generate a Christian identity. How does one achieve that when local prostitutes, who have shaved their heads as their calling card, have accepted Christ? The dichotomy of having a prostitute sitting next to a wealthy former Jewish woman in a newly developing religion must have suffered a plethora of social issues. As anyone who has had to shave the head knows, it takes a while for the hair to return to an extended length. Does someone place their faith on hold until they possess the appropriate look? No. What about the woman who suffers from malnutrition, a condition that exerts an outward effect on hair, nails, and skin? Remember, Paul identifies the activities for women: praying and prophesying. Are women forbidden from praying until they have the right look? No. In an instant, our hearts can change toward God, but our outward appearance may take a while to eliminate the worldly ways.

Men do not suffer from the social criticism of hair loss, as do women. Even to this day, society rejects balding women at a considerably greater rate than balding men. Paul's solution to this dilemma was to compel women to look similar when praying and speaking for the Lord. If all women cover their heads, then the covering becomes *an equalizer* as they preach the Word and pray. Head coverings worn by Christian women granted an equal status among the other believers. It is critical to understand that Paul is not saying the women cannot preach.

> But every woman who prays or prophesies with her head uncovered dishonors her head, since that is one and the same as having her head shaved. So if a woman's head is not covered, her hair should be cut off. But if it is disgraceful for a woman to have her hair cut off or her head shaved, she should be covered.

1 Corinthians 11:5-6 (HCSB)

The women were to pray and prophesy in the community, just as men were. Paul is not denying the prominent role of women in the church and their ability to lead. Today with our ability to manage cleanliness, water treatments, sustained levels of nutritious food stocks; the issue with hair, skin, and nails is not as prevalent as it was in the 1st century; therefore, our hair is our covering.

The rest of the passage is about the family to whom a woman belongs. As Christians, we are a family as the body of Christ. Moreover, each of them belonged to an individual family, headed by a male, for that time's customs. Paul is providing an identity to women, *not* condemning them for *being* a woman. "For just as woman came from man, so man comes through woman, and all things come from God" (1 Corinthians 11:12, HCSB). Paul is acutely aware of the role of women in the bringing of salvation to the world. In this section, Paul is categorically bungling in his writing of the letter for our 21st Century minds to understand. Paul is not denying the role of women in the church, nor is he making them subservient to men. He is trying to steer this mix-matched group of people and place them together under the heading of Christian. He has to create the hierarchy just like you would in a business setting. Paul is not saying women cannot be in the hierarchy of the church. He is trying to persuade *the men* to actively participate in the teachings of the church. First Peter 2:4-5 explains that we, men and women alike are a priesthood of believers,

> As you come to him, the living stone-rejected by humans but chosen by God and precious to him-you also, like living stones are being built into a spiritual house to be a holy priesthood, offering spiritual sacrifices acceptable to God through Jesus Christ.
>
> 1 Peter 2:4-5 (NIV)

How is the Apostle Paul going to disseminate information if not all can be present to learn? Women were saddled with child-rearing because birth control was not chemically regulated or physically altered like it is today. The meetings did not have electronic sound systems available for all to hear the person speaking. Hence, when a youngster was upset and crying in the room, it was the mother who removed the child, so the rest of the attendees could hear the message. Moreover, in traditional Jewish settings, men sat in the center, and the women and children sat on the periphery during worship. The husband became responsible for retaining the information he learned and disseminating it to his family. This arrangement allowed for the home environment to act as a primary setting promoting far more advantageous learning for moms with little ones. First Timothy discusses this in detail with gross misinterpretation by the modern reader without performing an inquiry of first-century Roman laws implemented or historical events. The 21st-century reader tends to cherry-pick scripture rather than analyze scripture in its entirety.[17] It was never an issue of not educating the women on the Word of the Lord; rather, it was an *auditory* issue for all to hear about our Lord Jesus Christ.

For our sisters, burdened with the pain of society's rejection of them in their feminine essence, ask: where does the pain hurt? Persuade them to pinpoint where it hurts the most. Is it loneliness, lack of income, abuse, no voice, and burdened with tasks? Whatever it is, coax them to identify the pain. Indicate from the beginning God listened to a woman's testimony. Only through the willingness of a young woman, Mary, to serve our preeminent God could God save the earth. Because God respected the feminine side of humanity's heart, God redeemed man. An authentic church in Christ not only appreciates the value of women but encourages leadership roles of women within its domination. In Christ, women acquire value. A start to the conversation would be the Gospel of Luke, where the author Luke shows Jesus' compassion to our humanity.

Hinduism—the sea of humanity and all living things melt together for one existence. Humanity is lower than all the gods and is ignorant to ourselves. There is "the one" god, the ultimate reality from which all of humanity descends in its inferior form. This deity is impersonal, but the qualities and characteristics can be identified through the manifestations of lesser gods. Karma plays a critical role in the afterlife and your reincarnation; we are all merely recycled beings. Dharma is your purpose in life, which could be the same as all your relatives. Man is born indebted to the gods, and throughout life, the penalty of payment must be made. To break the bondage of bad Karma, one must work to improve the outcome. People can work their entire life without knowing their life progress. How does one know when he/she is doing well enough to alter their karma? Do you find out when you are in your next life?

People are in a stuck existence without any way to assess one's performance. Therefore, a Hindu is habitually experiencing a life that denies the current life so that the subsequent life is more enjoyable. They fervently invoke and honor lesser gods in the hope of change. Yet, they will never know the outcome of that hope until death has come. One can go to the priest for guidance, but it is only the priests' interpretation of the sacred Veda texts. How does a Hindu know a priest's interpretation is authentic?

There are around one billion Hindus in the world today[18] that are feverishly working to gain a worthier life in the next life. What a heart-breaking existence. Our God has provided all things, so our works can never purchase His love for us. Why trust in a god that does not lessen the workload? The people are merely slaves to the cycle of reincarnation, always praying for a different outcome. Christ offers the hope of an end to the workload. Christ eases our burdens. With God, we secure our outcome before our death arrives. In the end, we know where and how we will reside. Our cherished Hindu friends need our Christian help to reveal to them the value within themselves to exchange their lives for a rest in Jesus. Because of all the testimonies found in the book of Acts, this would be an encouraging start for a new relationship with our Lord.

Judaism—to our cousins in faith, my heart aches for the Jewish to put the pieces of the true story together using the Old Testament. There are so many places where Jesus fulfills the scriptures about the Messiah. I pray scales to fall off their eyes and unlock their hearts to the beauty of how Jesus was the truth. I hear of record numbers of our Jewish friends believing in the savior Yeshua, which is such a blessing to the world. Those who are Messianic (Jews who believe in Jesus) are doing a great job teaching and praying for their Jewish friends within their communities. Unfortunately, Christians still have far more work to do. Matthew 10:5-6 (HCSB) states, "Jesus sent out these twelve after giving them instructions: 'Don't take the road leading to other nations, and don't enter any Samaritan town. Instead, go to the lost sheep of the house of Israel.'" Jesus started His message with the Jews first and then to the Gentiles. He worked so hard to correct the wayward spiritual ship of the Israelites. For our Jewish friends and family, we can delve deep into scripture, advancing line by line, revealing how there are 351 prophecies fulfilled by Jesus' birth, suffering, death, and resurrection.[19]

Get to know your Old Testament by exploring it. Christians have a tendency to only lean into the New Testament. In fact, it is in the Old Testament where Jesus begins His story for us. There is a Christian phrase that needs to be kept close to heart when teaching our Jewish friends about Jesus. "The Old Testament is the New Testament concealed; the New Testament is the Old Testament revealed."

Sad to relate, many Christians are reluctant to talk about Jesus to our Jewish friends, much like Moses was reluctant to go to his adoptive brother, Pharaoh, and forewarn him of impending death. Start with a cup of coffee or tea and open up your Bible to Isaiah 53 with your Jewish friend. Read out loud the scripture and then begin to connect the dots. This is Jesus' story. There are eyewitnesses to every step of His ministry, Jew and Gentile alike, documented in the New Testament. The Old Testament proclaims Jesus repeatedly. Isaiah 9:6 (HCSB): "For a child will be born for us, a son will be given to us, and the government will be on His shoulders. He will be named Wonderful Counselor, Mighty God, Eternal Father, Prince of Peace." Even secular sources, such as Josephus, documented the historical existence of Jesus' life and death.

We have to prove to our friends that Jesus came in peace first and not as a warrior. His trial and crucifixion tell us He was a man of Peace. Even the thief on the cross proclaimed Jesus's innocence. First Peter 2:22-23 (NLT) declares, "He never sinned, nor ever deceived anyone. He did not retaliate when insulted, nor threaten revenge when he suffered. He left his case in the hands of God, who always judges fairly." Just before His last breath, Jesus begins reciting Psalm 22. The Psalms are typically ascribed by the Jewish for words of comfort, encouragement, lamenting, and the such. "Even though some of the language or images may seem alien when one digs deep enough, one may find wellsprings of great impact."[20] Why did Jesus choose Psalm 22 at his death? Because Psalm 22 is a mirror image of Jesus and His life.

Be kind with your words to our Jewish friends. They have spent decades defending their faith and their land. Since our Jewish friends know considerably more about what Christians call the "Old Testament," we can glean volumes of New Testament information based on what our "faith cousins" can teach us. Take what knowledge they have in the Torah and deliver them to Jesus. More importantly, *learn together.*

Muslim— For this section, I will rely heavily on my experience in Indonesia, which is the largest Muslim country in the world. Muslim is the faith, and Islam comprises the political component of the religion. Just like Christianity and Judaism, the Muslim religion has many denominations or sects. These sects include people from indispensable medical missionaries to ultra-conservative political leaders and a plethora of other occupations. Addressing the Muslim religion is a touchy subject nowadays, but the people are worth being saved. Seen as a prophet, many Muslims want to know more about Jesus and the work He accomplished. Many Muslims are prolific in their apologetics, and we, in turn, must know and respond with our Christian apologetics. Recognize a healthy debate can transform a life to Jesus. With your conversation, try taking the Muslim from the prophet Jesus to the savior Jesus.

When we lived in Indonesia, Christmas was an incredibly personal time for us. We were not in a Christian country, even though Christians did live there and openly celebrated the holiday. Indonesia was once a Dutch colony, and therefore some of the Dutch traditions remained. When my dad read Luke 2 on Christmas Eve to the family (sometimes by kerosene light because there was no electricity), I momentarily experienced what the new Christians in the initial years endured. Early Christianity was an unwanted and undesired religion in a culture dominated by polytheistic religions and governmental leaders in the first couple of centuries after Christ's death. Radical anti-Christians in Indonesia were involved in an ample share of priestly beheadings and burning of Christian churches when we lived there, but it never stopped our belief. In fact, our church was constantly under bomb threats. We ignored a great many because the threats were weak. Yet sometimes the threats were very real, resulting in canceling of Sunday services. The opposition did not quite understand that the threats caused a counter-effect; they increased our faith and drove us deeper into the Bible.

Every year we would put up our Christmas tree, and our Muslim friends and house help would be incredibly curious about the meaning of the practice. Christmas is a delightful place to start when sharing Jesus with a Muslim. (Easter, in some ways, is a more emotional spiritual event for Christians, but the Christmas message provides wonderful visuals for those who know nothing about Jesus.) As a girl, I would discover the people who helped in our house looking intently at our Christmas tree. They tremendously enjoyed the lighted tree at night just as much as we did. As they viewed the ornaments, we would explain what each was and why it was significant. Moreover, we took the time to enlighten our Muslim friends about Jesus' birth and why God came to earth to deliver humanity from evil. Did any of our Muslim friends come to Christ? I do not know. I know we definitely generated a multitude of questions in their minds. One must realize the threat of hell constitutes an *absolutely real threat* to them, as well as a possible physical threat from the Muslim community. Many are forbidden to partake in anything Christian beyond seeking out basic information to affirm the Muslim religion. We need to have a great deal of patience with our Muslim friends and neighbors because Jesus has to overcome authentic fear in their hearts and minds.

I remember when my mom was providing a new employer for our cook, Leila, because we were preparing to return to the United States. My parents worked hard to acquire gainful employment for all those who helped in our house so they could carry on with their lives after our departure. (Their families and responsibilities were not absolved once we left.) My mom asked Leila her preferences for her next employer. She preferred a job with someone in the American or Dutch embassy. My mom inquired why, since most embassy personnel salary is low and therefore pay lesser amounts to the local hires. Although she could obtain a high-paid position with an affluent Muslim family, Leila desired to work for a Christian family. Amazed at her employment wish, my mom again asked why. Leila responded even though she might receive more money from a local wealthy Muslim family, she preferred the Christian families because they regarded her and her family better. Chuckling to herself, my mom blurted out with a twinkle in her eye, "Leila, admit it. You are a Christian!" Leila smiled an ever-slight smile and said, "No, I just prefer working for Christians." You see, if Leila professed Christianity, she would have to face her family and community at home, and that would have been too great of a physical risk. I pray for Leila's faith walk to this day.

As Christians, we need to recognize the *people* who are Muslim and where they can use Jesus in their lives. Pray for them when they have sickness and disease. Support them when tragedy strikes and ask, "Do you know Jesus?" From their superficial knowledge of Jesus as a prophet, teach them Jesus is God. A single God came to this earth to die for us because He is fully merciful and fully just. The Christian God is *both* merciful and just because He sacrificed himself as an innocent man, taking on all the sins of the world. Otherwise, someone loses in the sentencing by God—either the person begging for mercy or the person begging for justice.

For example, if there was a robbery and a person was murdered during the event. During the trial, the victims of the crime demand justice, and the perpetrator pursues mercy. Only through a God who walked on this earth, who committed no crime, killed, and rose from the grave, can offer both mercy *and* justice simultaneously. God maintains justice for the robber in that he must stand before Him and confess his sin. By his confession, the robber receives a sentence for punishment for the crime. This is justice. But if the robber accepts Jesus into his life, implores forgiveness, and changes how he spends his life, mercy is given; since the punishment was carried out by Christ's innocent death on the cross. Christ on the cross becomes the proxy for the punishment we should receive. This is mercy.

Moreover, God desires you to know when you die where you are going to spend eternity. Your end destination in eternity should not remain a guessing game. Fraught with worry, the faithful learn of their permanent home based on Allah's decision on judgment day. How do you know if Allah is having a good day or a terrible day when he sentences you? On judgment day, our Muslim friends have to hope all their judged work in the five pillars during their life on earth is on a good day for Allah; otherwise, there is no heaven for them.

There is much comfort in knowing God wants you *with* Him when you cross over. Our God instructed Moses to inscribe His words for the people to follow. The writings of the prophets, the Kings, and the struggles of the Israelites throughout the area are all true. God's book has not been corrupted. Proof of this is discovered in all the archeological artifacts and excavations that are currently happening within the borders of Israel today. Over and over again, archeological findings are an exact match for the stories in the Old Testament. In addition, many of the people like myself who have received near-death experiences confirm what the Bible says: Jesus, God, and the Holy Spirit are the one Triune God who adores His children.

What I witnessed among the Muslim community towards women, in general, is heartbreaking at best. Adolescent girls with limited education were offered to older men as second and third wives. Seen as a financial burden, pre-teen girls were given away in arranged marriages to alleviate family expenses. Indonesia in the 1970s was a developing country and newly independent from the Dutch. Males obtained a compulsory sixth-grade education; however, females only needed to attend up to the fifth grade in public schools. There were opportunities for students to further their education beyond the mandated grade level, but usually that was at an exorbitant personal expense. With the country under economic stress, the average parent could not afford to send their children to higher levels of school. Child labor after the age of twelve was prolific.

Based on my personal experience, I consider the Muslim religion and its sharia laws are remarkably pro-men and extraordinarily unfair to women. Jesus liberates women into what God intended them, with all the rights and responsibilities of having an authentic and authoritative voice. He frees women from the bondage of cloth and loss of identity. Jesus came for all people in the world to include our Muslim friends and neighbors. We must be in fervent prayer for our Muslim friends. As Christians, we need to show kindness so that they are free to worship the God of love and salvation. A God who is fully merciful and fully justified through the cross of Jesus Christ. A fantastic beginning in a new faith walk for our kind-hearted Muslim friends would be the Gospel of John.

Occult—the secretiveness of this religion surrounds its believers in darkness. Peppered with ceremonies, rituals, seances, and sacrifices, Satanism, Voodoo, and the like thrive in a mysterious world. The sorcery uses secret chants and spells to control and expel those opposed to their belief, economics, or political gain. The blood fulfills a critical role in achieving objectives. My personal exposure to the occult is extremely limited to what I have discovered from my former students. From my understanding, there is the information cult members can discuss, then there is a considerably deeper level of information. The darker level of information reserved for specific members at higher levels is forbidden discussion outside the religion. Everything is secretly done so that information is managed and skillfully measured, relying heavily on pain and suffering for control.

For our friends raised in the occult religions, petition them about the light. Compel them to describe what the light might look like. Occultists push people down into darkness, into entrapped fear and complete indoctrination of a lesser being. As Christians, we want to concentrate on the light, where God reveals all information to anyone who asks. The Christian's value rests on the image of a gracious and loving God. Opposite to the occult's teaching, death is not a viable end for those who wish for a worthier life. Truth in Jesus can dispel the anger, fear, hurt, and pain inflicted on oneself and towards others. Jesus' blood is the only blood needed for a life in eternal goodness. "...The Son of God came for this: to destroy the devil's work" (1 John 3:8, ERV). God does heed your cries of pain, anger, fear. God is aware of all things, and yet God still longs for your heart to cry out to Him for help. Urge them when they feel confused in their pain, and anger, or lack of control to call out to Jesus. In Matthew 10:27-28 (HCSB), Jesus says, "What I tell you in the dark, speak in the light. What you hear in a whisper, proclaim on the housetops. Don't fear those who kill the body but are not able to kill the soul; rather, fear Him who is able to destroy both soul and body in hell." Matthew 12:7 (ERV): "The Scriptures say, 'I don't want animal sacrifices; I want you to show kindness to people.' You don't really know what that means. If you understood it, you would not judge those who have done nothing wrong."

The academically challenged students I taught, those with no clear behavioral or developmental obstacles, were of keen interest to me. I never allowed them get away with substandard performance just to get away with it. I would call their behavior out. Pointing my finger at them, I would say, "So if you cannot be the best of the best, you are going to be the best of the worst. But no matter what, you are going to be the best at something. You want to win." They would look at me straight on, and after a silent moment, they would sheepishly agree with me. I never had one such student disagree with me, not one. Kids want to be good at something. People, in general, want to be good at something. They possess a desire to be the best at something because that provides them an identity. If they are not talented to keep up with the good ones, they will bust their butts working at being the best of the bad ones.

Many times, people fall into the occult as a way to dominate the "win." If a person feels they can never be talented enough, no matter how hard they try, slipping into the darkness of the occult can produce a pseudo-euphoria of being the best of the bad. This euphoria produces a problem of entrapment. They become trapped in the darkness and do not own any idea how to crawl out. They do not have a skill set that can focus on the light and love of God when they have grown fatigued and weary of the darkness. Moreover, these victims are threatened by religious members with loss of family, friends, and, yes, even their own life. The individuals who choose to leave the occult are courageous people who can at times feel quite lonely.

Jesus provides an identity, exactly what these adults and youngsters are seeking. Unfortunately, they have become caught in a spiraling descent of darkness in their quest for some sort of identity; whether through family influence, social media, social groups, TV, and movies. These are mightily broken individuals who require our help. Thankfully, there is an easier and healthier way to live a life. Jesus tells us He is the truth, the way, and the light in John 14:6.

As Christian, I would encourage humility and kindness to these individuals. Through the kindness of works and words, people deceived in the occult will begin trusting. Trust remains an *enormous* issue for these individuals because the devil is a liar. From trust, you can begin praying *with* them. Petition them directly if you can pray for them. Allow them to hear your words of concern for their well-being. The Holy Spirit has to show them a new identity, in the light of salvation from Satan's power and the possibility of God's wrath. I know people who have left this earthly darkness and come into the light. The gravest fear is God not fully forgiving them for all the wickedness that they have done to people and animals. "For he has rescued us from the kingdom of darkness and transferred us into the Kingdom of his dear Son" (Colossians 1:13, NLT). As Christians, we need to be there as they transfer their lives into the light of God. We pray for them. We pray to God to use His most powerful authority in handling demons when necessary. Caution is much-needed when confronting demonic possession, I must add. Do this with someone experienced who understands the levels of heaven and the strategic need for fasting and repentance. Never consider a situation without your heart being right with Jesus and proclaiming His name. Remember, God's team is the winning team.

We need to offer our friends a place at our Christian tables and feed them the Word, not expecting anything in return for the invite. Suggest to them scripture which shows when all believe and repent of their sins, they will be saved no matter what of their past life practices. Jesus knocked Paul off his horse riding to Damascus as he was hunting down Christians to execute, and yet our wonderfully loving God found favor with him. All who believe and repent are given life eternal. This is the hope of Jesus Christ, and it is obtainable for them just like it is obtainable for everyone else. For our worthy friends trapped in darkness, the book of Romans and the Gospel of John are wonderfully written to bring them the good news of Jesus Christ.

Paganism—regaining in popularity Paganism such as Wicca, Druidism, and Norsemen comprise a category of religion that honors nature, believing its elements contain spiritual beings. Blockbuster movies and popular television shows have contributed to the growth of these pagan religions. Knowledge is power. Control of the earth and its elements offer satisfaction of personal accomplishment. Life, in all its forms, possess a valuation determined by the religion. Like most religions, they utilize a calendar that represents various elements to celebrate. Mayday, Halloween, the Solstices' celebrations and the like are all a dynamic part of the ritual calendar glamorized by Hollywood. Many believe when the early Christian church began developing its calendar, it relied heavily on the existing pagan celebrations. I disagree, since many important Christian days are directly mirrored from the Jewish calendar.

Cases-in-point: Easter and Christmas. Christmas is not a substitute for the winter solstice, as some may believe. Solstices are celebrated on the 19th, 20th, or 21st, depending on the year and if it is a leap or not. Christmas is persistently on the 25th of December, paralleling Hanukkah (aka, the winter Feast of Dedication or the Festival of Lights), of which Jesus celebrated in the Gospel of John.

"And it was at Jerusalem, the feast of the dedication, and it was winter" (John 10:22, HCSB). Biblical scholars cannot identify the precise date of Jesus' birth, but we celebrate His birth during the time of Hanukkah. As Christians, we rejoice in the Light of the World who walked on the earth and enjoy a dedicated celebration that reflects the Jewish Festival of Lights. Furthermore, St. Nicolas, the 4th Century Bishop of Myra, is in heaven for his dedicated and passionate work for the poor and downtrodden. He was a devoted servant of our Lord Jesus Christ, a person in Christendom that the faithful should emulate. "Santa Claus," the fictional character based on St. Nicolas, is a retail marketing department's promotional stunt that comes at the end of a massive parade.

The Easter egg has been implemented in Christendom since the beginning. Early Christians debated on the timing of the Easter celebration: annually on Passover or weekly? The fallout from that exchange confirms that by about AD 160, the Christian community had adopted a distinct annual celebration.[21] In keeping with some Jewish traditions practiced in the first century, the egg was adopted into Christianity from the Passover plate. "The *Beitzah* (egg) represents the festival of sacrifice and is a symbol of Spring."[22] As a visual aid in the retelling of the resurrection, Christians chose to dye the egg red to represent the blood shed on the cross. In fact, many Orthodox Christians dye the Easter egg red to this day. Regrettably, western cultures have overtaken Easter for profit, and food dye companies have used this holiday to promote multiple colors. Christmas and the Easter egg are just two examples where gross miscommunication and a lack of understanding abound when comparing paganism with Christianity.

Paganism is polytheistic in composition, relying on gods (Odin, Thor, Mother Nature, etc.) and enchanted beings (fairies, elves, and the such) which interact with people for a specific purpose. Moreover, paganism is not about suppression of oneself; rather, it is about ceremonies, rituals, and spells that rely heavily on symbolism that assist them in their quest for knowledge of all things within the universe.[23] At its core, paganism is about receiving what *you* want out of life by summoning power through the earth or the universe for a desired result. Merely wave a wand, cast a spell, and your first-grade teacher becomes a frog. Whammo! Instant gratification!

I have known several pagans (Druids and Wiccans) who were wonderfully peaceful people, curious about what nature has to offer. Their love for the Earth is commendable. For our pagan friends, it is advantageous to bridge the gap between God and gods. They display a wholesome respect for nature and the supernatural, so God as our Creator is not a foreign concept to comprehend; it is just one that needs clarification and redirection.

Our heavenly Father warns against loving the earth more than the earth's Creator in the book of Deuteronomy. Specifically, our God warns about tampering in the supernatural. "No one among you is to make his son or daughter pass through the fire, practice divination, tell fortunes, interpret omens, practice sorcery, cast spells, consult a medium or a familiar spirit or inquire of the dead" (Deuteronomy 18:10, HCSB). Popular books, cartoons, movies, television shows, even theme parks promote magic or demi-god superpower, which conditions today's youth to accept the role of a lesser godly power as a considerable influence in the outcome of life.

God's design is a magnificent, multifaceted creation of many realms, seen and unseen, which does *not* rely on magic tricks, spells, or a minor god's superpower. Heaven and heavenly beings are able to interact with us all the time at God's discretion; none of us is an island unto our own. Interconnected with multiple dimensions, we are all created by our all-powerful God. Jesus served as the perfect illustration of how these worlds interact when He returned from the grave and spoke with Mary and His disciples. In addition, God spoke directly to Adam and Eve in the garden. Jacob witnessed angels ascending and descending on a ladder from heaven.

As challenging as it is to read, all the world's knowledge is and has been available in the Bible. God has never withheld any knowledge from us. If we ask, we will receive in His time. (Might I emphasize "...*in His time*".) "That's how we know we belong to the way of truth. And when our hearts make us feel guilty, we can still have peace before God, because God is greater than our hearts. He knows everything" (1 John 3:19-20, ERV).

There is no need for an incantation to talk to Jesus, just a heart to learn about Him and fall in love with Him. Thor's hammer does *not* control anything. The Christian God is above *all* that is created. There is no rock, no mountain, no body of water, no heaven that God cannot hold in the palm of His hand. Our God is a God outside of creation, and no manipulation by anything created can supersede the creator's will. Our one God is so much bigger than the multiple pagan gods. Why not worship the mightiest God that governs all things, rather than smaller gods who "control" only specific elements of creation? John the Baptist answered his disciples when they questioned Jesus' activities on the other side of the Jordan River, "No one can receive a single thing unless it's given to him from heaven" (John 3:27, HCSB). John is openly confessing to his team of followers that Jesus is Godly sent; He is *The Messiah*. Why not follow the big guy rather than follow a bunch of little guys? Have confidence that the Holy Spirit will provide a better and more compelling message than any hope in a lesser god. For our natured-hearted Pagan friends, the book of Acts shows the power and might of the Holy Spirit which provides a wealth of information for their new journey in Christ.

The Dream

"No prophecy ever came from what some person wanted to say. But
people were led by the Holy Spirit and spoke words from God."
1 Peter 1:21 (ERV)

Like most people, I dream at night. Sometimes my very well-organized dreams progress from ordered step to ordered step, each scene completely in sync. The colors and characters are vivid, and the stories are remarkably coherent. When I wake from this type of dream, I remember in detail the steps and images. Although a normal dream for me consists of a mash of images and activities that relate together no more than the Eiffel Tower and peanut butter on a race track—I pay attention when I have the dreams of order and specificity. I have learned to write these orderly dreams down and seek God to illustrate for me what I must comprehend or convey to others.

A couple of years ago, I had a dream that placed my heart on a fast track. In my dream, I was backstage climbing the back stairs of a theater stage, much like a performer waiting for their cue to step into the stage lights and begin their part in a well-rehearsed play. The vast, dark-navy velvet curtains hanging from the ceiling and partitioning the backstage from the stage's wood floor were heavy and blocked all stage light. Two lines of people were ascending the backstage steps. People were silent and reverent as they waited. My two daughters were with me in line, quietly anxious for our turn at the top of the steps. An exceptionally tall angel, about twelve feet tall, dressed in jeans and a plaid shirt and looking very much like a lumberjack, was standing in between the two admission lines, purposely allowing only one person from each line to proceed onto the stage area. Slowly and methodically, we ascended each step, one by one, waiting for our granted entrance on the heavily polished wood stage floor.

As my family and I reached the top three steps, I turned to the angel and observed him as he drew the curtains back to allow the next person in each of the lines to enter. (I was thinking, *hmmm, how come he is dressed in jeans and a plaid shirt and not a white robe? And just where does an angel that tall get jeans that size?*) He then quickly closed the curtains before the following person in line could walk on the stage. Everyone before me, quietly and reverently, respected the angel's authority in his role as an usher.

I stepped on the top step as the person in front of me entered the back of the stage. The angel looked at me (not speaking with his mouth, only with his eyes and gestures) and beckoned me to step closer to the curtain to proceed through it. With a twinkle in his eye, the angel drew the curtain back with his left hand and gestured with his massive right hand to proceed onto the stage. I looked around the curtain and saw the stage set with bright stage lights. The show was "on", and I was to accept my place at center stage in the intensely bright lights and then move into the arena where there were billions upon billions of people waiting for the glory of God to arrive.

Things were opposite a normal stage arrangement. Although one by one, we initially entered the stage area and stood in the stage lights, we proceeded to walk to the back of the crowd of billions anticipating the Glory of the Lord. The area where the sea of humanity was waiting extended farther than my eyes could see; I could not describe it in earthly terms. I returned my gaze to the angel and said to him, "There is not much room." He nodded ever so gently in agreement. I looked back into the room and saw there was only a small sliver of space in the back of the crowd for the rest of us. The room was overcapacity, "standing room only" for those of us late in the game. I turned back to the angel and said, "It is almost full." His eyes had lost the twinkle, and he bestowed on me a look of confirmation as he nodded in agreement. Realizing that heaven is near capacity with minimal space left, I asked the angel if my two daughters could go on ahead of me. Again, he nodded in agreement.

Once I had made sure my girls were safely at the back of the crowd, I turned to the angel and asked, "How much time?" He responded with, "Not much. Go quickly." As I raced down the steps, I noticed the angel began denying specific individuals' entrance on the stage. The people became horrified since they thought they would receive automatic admission. The angel was using his vast size to repel any attempts of intrusion as they tried gaining entrance behind the curtain. Their tears of anguish were heart-wrenching. Hearing their screams and shouts as they tried fighting the angel's decision was terrifying. I can remember thinking, *Oh no! They are not getting in! They thought they were going to get in, and they are denied. Now I know why the angel is so big.* I instantly understood the angel's permanent decision in the screaming cacophony of the forbidden.

During my descent, I could tell that, although at the beginning, refusal was only to the few, the further I went down the stairs, more and more were denied. In the end, scarcely any in each line were granted permission to step on stage. It was as if I could read the hearts and minds of the rejected as I descended the long staircase. The people honestly thought they were good people and that their "goodness" should grant them automatic admission. Much like the sinking Titanic with only a few lifeboats for the many aboard the ship, only the select few were saved, while the rest were left to struggle for their final breath.

Knowing that earth would soon be destroyed, I proceeded to race down the long backstage staircase between the two lines of humanity. After my long descent, I found myself back into the world of the hustle and bustle firmly on a sidewalk. My breath caught in the back of my throat as I recognized people's ominous status. My mission was to warn people that time is almost up; heaven has very little room left. The curtain will promptly close for eternity. People thinking they are faithful Christians will cross over into the darkness or, worse, hell. No matter how good people think they are, it is not good enough. *You must fall in love with Jesus and regard Him as Lord of your life.* My dream impressed upon me that I have to share the truth about Jesus and what He completed for the world before it is too late.

Please dedicate your life to Jesus! You are considered worthy if you indeed believe that God walked on this earth for you. God loves you and desires you with Him in heaven. Believe He died and rose to provide you the marvelous gift of eternal life to you. Repent of your earthly ways. There is so much more to life than just what is here on earth. Please, I firmly believe there is no more time! The time on the one-hand clock is about to expire. Where is your eternity? You can prefer the light and escape the darkness.

The Prayer

"...'O God, be merciful to me, for I am a sinner.' I tell you, this sinner,
not the Pharisee, returned home justified before God..."
Luke 18:13-14 (NLT)

Dear God, Holy Triune Father, who created us for your use and your will, we come to you today not because we need our wants fulfilled but rather because we recognize you as THE Father of all living things. From all things you own comes all that we have and all that we need. We pray for all leaders in our communities, small and great, to lead by example, as Christ leads all of us by His example. For those of us unsure just what this life is about, we seek that purpose be placed on their hearts. Our friends hurting from actions or words of others, we ask for a comforted heart and strength to stand up for the goodness inside. For those of us who are lost and require reassurance in our steps to Christ, we beseech you to regain our footing in your Word and repent of our sins. Those of us who designate ourselves as the people of God, may we humble ourselves and abhor all earthly ways. May we be encouraged to lift our hands in prayer to You, never-ceasing in public reading, teaching, and encouraging others in the Word. Uncover our eyes, ears, and minds in prophetic knowledge, then open our mouths to proclaim Your prophecy until the day of Jesus' return. Regulate our speech and behavior into a holy illustration. Let us be unafraid to lay hands on the ill, cast out demons, and intercede for those compromised in economic misfortune. May we pray for all people, delivered and undelivered. Let us practice all the spiritual gifts You have given to us. Save us all from the darkness and the chaos to come on the earth. May we love our neighbors and our families as we forgive all the wrongs we suffer at the hands of others. Only through the blood of Jesus and the resurrected body can Your mercy and justice prevail. May the will of the people represent only Your divine will. We pray this in the name of Jesus Christ. Amen.

"Come to me, all you who are weary and burdened,
and I will give you rest"
Matthew 11:28 (NIV)

Bibliography

Bible League International. *The Gateway Bible.com.* 2006. https://biblegateway.com.

Akin, Daniel L. *Five who changed the world.* Wake Forest: Southeastern Baptist Theological Seminary, 2008.

Barr, Beth Allison. *The Making of Biblical Womanhood.* Grand Rapids: BrazosPress, 2021.

Boom, Corrie Ten. *The Hiding Place, 35th anniversary edition.* Grand Rapids: Cosen Books, 1971.

"Complementarianism." *Theopedia.com.* n.d. https://www.theopedia.com/complementarianism (accessed April 9, 2021).

Galli, Mark. 131 *Christian Everyone Should Know.* Nashville: B&H Publishing House, 2000.

We Were Soliders. Directed by Randall Wallace. Performed by Mel Gibson. 2002.

Hinduism. March 22, 2017. http://www.religionfacts.com/hinduism (accessed August 13, 2019).

Holman Bible Publishers. *Holy Bible The Old and New Testaments HCSB.* Nashville: Holman Bible Publishers, 2016.

Jonsson, Patrik. *The Christian Science Monitor.* February 3, 2010. https://www.csmonitor.com/USA/Society/2010/0203/Top-5-Tim-Tebow-eye-black-biblical-verses (accessed March 6, 2021).

Judith A. Berling. *Confucianism.* n.d. https://asiasociety.org/education/confucianism (accessed August 13, 2019).

Margery S. Berube. *The American Heritage Dictionary.* Boston: Dell Publishing, 1983.

—. *The American Heritage Dictionary.* New York: Dell Publishing, 1983.

Peers, E. Allison. *St. John of the Cross, Dark Knight of the Soul.* Mineola: Dover Publications, Inc., 2003.

Pelaia, Ariela. ""Lilith, from the Medieval Period to Modern Feminist Texts."" *Learn Religions.* 2020 26, Aug. https://www.learnreligions.com/the-legend-of-lilith-2076653 (accessed April 2, 2021).

Quinn, Shannon. *History Collection*. n.d. https://historycollection.co/operation-pied-piper-the-mass-evacuation-of-children-in-london-during-wwii/ (accessed August 5, 2019).

Reform Judaism. "ReformJudaism.org." *Reform Judaism*. 2021. https://reformjudaism.org/jewish-holidays/passover/learn-about-passover-seder-plate (accessed March 31, 2021).

Schoolworkhelper. n.d. https://schoolworkhelper.net/pagan-rituals-and-beliefs/ (accessed August 16, 2019).

Shelley, Bruce L. *Church History in Plain Language*. Nashville: Thomas Nelson, 2013.

Stern, David H. *Complete Jewish Bible*. Clarksville: Jewish New Testament Publications, 1998.

It's A Wonderful Life. Directed by Frank Capra. Performed by Jimmy Stewart. 1946.

Strong, James. *The New Strong's Expanded Exhaustive Concordance of the Bible*. Nashville: Thomas Nelson Publishers, 2010.

Webb, David. *New Testament Christians.com*. April 25, 2013. http://www.newtestamentchristians.com/bible-study-resources/351-old-testament-prophecies-fulfilled-in-jesus-christ/ (accessed August 14, 2019).

Weintraub, Rabbi Simkha Y. *My Jewish Learning.com*. n.d. https://www.myjewishlearning.com/article/psalms-as-prayer/ (accessed August 14, 2019).

Wilson, Keith J. "The Christian History and Development of Easter," in Celebrating Easter: The 2006 BYU Easter Conference, ed." *Religious Studies Center, Brigham Young University*. 2006. https://rsc.byu.edu/celebrating-easter/christian-history-development-easter (accessed April 3, 2021).

Zondervan. *The Holy Bible International Version,* Archaeological Study Bible. Grand Rapids: Zondervan, 2005.

The Holy Bible, New International Version. Grand Rapids: MI, 2005.

The Holy Bible, New Living Translation. Grand Rapids: Zondervan, 2005.

Endnotes

[1] (Stewart 1946)

[2] (Galli 2000 p.268-270)

[3] (Peers 2003 p.4)

[4] (Shelley 2013 p.249)

[5] (Stern 1998 p.xxxiii)

[6] (Gibson 2002)

[7] (Boom 1971 p.87-88)

[8] (Jonsson 2010)

[9] (Quinn n.d.)

[10] (Bible League International 2006, footnote)

[11] (Akin 2008 p.72)

[12] (Akin 2008 p.75)

[13] (Margery S. Berube 1983)

[14] (Judith A. Berling n.d.)

[15] (Complementarianism n.d.)

[16] (Pelaia Aug)

[17] (Barr 2021, p.58)

[18] (Hinduism 2017)

[19] (Webb 2013)

[20] (Weintraub n.d.)

[21] (Wilson 2006)

[22] (Reform Judaism 2021)

[23] (Schoolworkhelper n.d.)